LEON MORRIS

The Abolition of Religion

———

A STUDY IN
'RELIGIONLESS CHRISTIANITY'

LONDON
INTER-VARSITY FELLOWSHIP
39 BEDFORD SQUARE, W.C.1

© The Inter-Varsity Fellowship
First Edition . . *May, 1964*
Reprinted . . *September, 1965*

Made and printed in England by
STAPLES PRINTERS LIMITED
at their Rochester, Kent, establishment

CONTENTS

ABBREVIATIONS

BR: *Beyond Religion,* by Daniel Jenkins (London, 1962).

Four Anchors: *Four Anchors from the Stern,* ed. Alan Richardson (London, 1963).

Letters: *Letters and Papers from Prison,* by D. Bonhoeffer (Fontana Books, 1959).

HTG: *Honest to God,* by John A. T. Robinson, Bishop of Woolwich (London, 1963).

HTGD: *The Honest to God Debate,* ed. David L. Edwards (London, 1963).

PREFACE

ONE of the stimulating things about the debate that has followed the publication of the Bishop of Woolwich's *Honest to God* is the awakening of interest in what is termed 'religionless Christianity'. This is not a new concept, first put out by the Bishop. Rather it is an important and interesting idea previously held, but now more widely known. My aim in this book is to study some aspects of this 'religionless Christianity'.

As Dietrich Bonhoeffer and Bishop Robinson have written most persuasively about it I have perforce had to concentrate a good deal on their writings. But I want it to be clear that my concern is with 'religionless Christianity' and not with any particular exponent of it. I am not able to accept the idea, at least as it has so far been expressed. But it is altogether too simple, in my judgment, either to accept it whole-heartedly or to reject it out of hand. I find much that its exponents have said to be profitable. I am sure that the orthodox ought to engage in a good deal of heart-searching. The new writers are surely right in rebuking them about much in the way they have understood the faith and also in the way they have presented it to others. We ought to be provoked by them to think out afresh the meaning and the implications of Christianity. As far as I am able this is what I have tried to do.

I am fairly sure that I shall be accused of misinterpreting or misunderstanding both Dietrich Bonhoeffer and the Bishop of Woolwich, so I want to say in advance this is not intentional. But in the writings of both I have found what seem to me to be contradictory ideas, ideas which I see no way of harmonizing, and which I do not think the authors have harmonized. Sometimes they appear to be very radical, sometimes quite conservative.

I have not always felt it necessary, when dealing with these contradictory ideas, to quote passages dealing with both aspects. To have done this would have made my little book much longer, and would have meant introducing so many qualifications as to have made the argument even harder to follow than it is now. I have simply assumed that the authors will stand by what they have said, and have selected passages which seem to me important. If I have made a wrong selection, I am sorry.

It remains only for me to express my indebtedness to those who have written on the theme before me. As I have read and thought I have learned a great deal to my profit. It is my hope that this little book will help others to see some of the issues a little more clearly and that, whether they find themselves able to agree with me or not, they will be provoked into thinking again over what it is that Christians are called to believe and to do.

LEON MORRIS

CHAPTER ONE

OBJECTIONS TO 'RELIGION'

THE term 'religionless Christianity' has enjoyed
a certain popularity in theological writing in
recent days. It is not easy to define, all the more so
since those who use the term are not perfectly agreed on
what it denotes (we shall return to this point). It may
accordingly be too much to speak of a 'school of thought',
but there is a recognizable similarity of emphasis in a
number of recent writings. J. A. T. Robinson's *Honest
to God* has caught the public imagination, and it may
serve as an outstanding example of the general trend.
But we must not overlook the fact that the Bishop of
Woolwich confesses himself to be heavily indebted to
the writings of such men as Dietrich Bonhoeffer and Paul
Tillich, or that he cites John Wren-Lewis and others of
similar outlook. We see something of the same trend in
Daniel Jenkins' *Beyond Religion*, in R. Gregor Smith's
The New Man, and in the composite volumes produced
recently by Cambridge theologians, *Soundings*, and
Objections to Christian Belief. Dr. Robinson mentions
also Werner Pelz, *God is No More*, John Taylor, *The
Primal Vision: Christian Presence amid African Religion*,
Sir Richard Acland, *We Teach Them Wrong: Religion
and the Young*, and Paul van Buren, *The Secular Meaning of the Gospel*.

It is clear that there is sufficient interest in this subject
to make it worthy of careful study. It is equally clear
that, while the expression may vary from one writer to
another, there is a recognizable pattern emerging from
these various writings, though the similarity is greater in
some aspects of the faith than in others. This pattern
witnesses to a movement of theological thought which

7

must be taken seriously. It will certainly demand a great deal of attention from all who are concerned with Christian thinking and Christian living for quite some time to come.

In this present study we are not concerned with all the aspects of a book like *Honest to God*. Rather our concern is with the claim that 'religion' and Christianity are rightly to be distinguished, and that we should reject the former in the interests of the latter. If this is true the implications for our understanding of the faith are far-reaching. They are so far-reaching that much that is traditional both in our understanding of the faith and in our practice of Christian living will require radical modi-fication. Therefore it is important for us to think carefully about what we are offered.

As a general rule, throughout the centuries, Christians have thought that religion was integral to their way of life. 'The Christian Religion' is an accepted expression, and most of us have never felt it was something to apologize for or to be called in question. Quite often, it is true, people have tried to distinguish between genuine Christianity and a mere outward profession, and they have sometimes used the term 'religion' as a way of describing the latter. In this sense of the term we would all be convinced that 'religionless Christianity' is highly desirable.

But it is not at all clear that this is what recent writers have in mind. The criticisms now being offered affect not only that type of religion which is merely formal and outward, but also a good deal which goes deeper. Indeed it would scarcely be an exaggeration to say that the religious man is now being regarded as more likely to be wrong than to be right. His very religion is seen as a human mechanism, a defence erected to enable him to resist the claims of God.

It is obviously a point common to most of the writers whom we have in mind that they regard 'religion' as

something to be abhorred. And, since this view is something of a novelty in Christianity, we must give close
attention to what is understood by 'religion'. It is not at
all certain that we are right in assuming that what we
commonly understand by 'religion', and hence, 'religionless', is what these new writers understand by the terms.
Alan Richardson thinks a good deal is due to mistrans-
lation from the German: 'if *religionslose* had been translated by some such English word as "unpietistic" or
"unchurchy", a good deal of unnecessary perplexity and
distress would have been spared.'[1] This may account for
some of the difficulty. If the Germans and the English
mean different things by 'religionless' then obviously there
will be a certain amount of confusion and we shall not
find it easy to understand what is written.

The confusion is furthered by another fact. The writers
of whom we are thinking do not usually explain exactly
what they mean by the term 'religion'. Dr. Robinson,
it is true, does recognize that 'much of the discussion for
and against "religion" is bound to be a matter of definition',[2] and he proceeds to cite a definition from Tillich.
Unfortunately, however, he does not accept the definition
for the purposes of discussion, preferring 'to retain the
customary usage'. But he never tells us what 'the customary usage' is.

It should moreover be borne in mind when Robinson
cites Tillich's definition that the latter is not rightly
classed as an upholder of 'religionless Christianity'. He is
giving a definition of 'religion' that he accepts, not one
that he castigates. If we are to find what the 'religion' is
that 'religionless Christianity' repudiates we are left
largely to our own devices.

It may help us to take four characteristics of religion
as Dietrich Bonhoeffer sees it. I take the following summary by Eberhard Bethge from Daniel Jenkins' book:
'First, it is individualistic. The religious man is pre-

[1] *Four Anchors*, p. 13.   [2] *HTG*, p. 86, n. 2.

occupied with himself and his interior states in such a way as to forget his neighbour, even though this individualism may take ascetic and apparently self-sacrificial forms. Secondly, it is metaphysical. God is brought in to complete, as the supernatural, a fundamentally man-centred view of reality. Thirdly, the religious interest becomes more and more one department of life only. Scientific discovery and other forces push it more and more into insignificant areas of life. And fourthly, the God of religion is a *deus ex machina,* one who comes in from the outside to help his children when they are in trouble. He is not the One at the centre of life, who controls and directs it and meets and sustains us in our strength as well as our weakness.'[3]

It is unlikely that Christians have ever intended to produce a 'religion' like this. Nevertheless it is beyond doubt that sometimes believers have left themselves open to all four criticisms. It is particularly easy to succumb to the first temptation, though we would never admit even to ourselves that this is what we are doing. But a man may come to regard his religious life as an affair in which he concerns himself with the needs of his own soul. He gives a good deal of attention to ensuring that he has times of prayer and of meditation over the Bible, times in which he worships God, times in which he hears sermons and lectures and is thus instructed in the religion which he professes to hold and in the way in which his own spiritual life may be deepened. He does not see others as people to be loved and served in their own right. Rather he sees them as fodder for conversion, or as people whom he can help along the way of life in the furtherance of his own spiritual well-being.

Now it is of course true that the Christian ought to be alert to try to bring others to conversion. And it is true that his service of others will help his own spiritual life. But it is wrong if either (or both!) of these activities is approached purely in terms of the Christian's own well-being. A man should try to bring others to Christ out of love for them and because it is right, and not because of any good or ill that it will do him personally. He should try to do good to his fellows for their sake, not his. It is fatally easy to be concerned basically with ourselves, with our own spiritual advancement, even in our most apparently altruistic and self-sacrificing moments.

It is no less true that Bonhoeffer's second, third and fourth points can be illustrated all too abundantly from the lives of many Christians. It is not that we say that life is man-centred, but that we live it that way. It is not that we affirm that religion is concerned with one aspect of life only, but that we apply religious tests to those activities which we regard as 'spiritual', while we pursue our studies in science, art, technology, and the rest, for all the world as though we were happy pagans. It is not that we deny that God is Lord of all of life. But so often we live our lives in such a way that we call upon God only, or mainly, in those situations when we are out of our depth.

'Man's extremity is God's opportunity' is a proverb which can be most misleading. It does, of course, convey a profound truth. No Christian would deny that God works wonderfully in situations where man is without resource. We have all seen this time and time again in our Christian experience. But the trouble is that the proverb can so easily be understood as though God were quiescent, a spectator in the affairs of life while man does everything within his power. Then when man has reached his extremity, and only when this point is reached, God steps in. This is undoubtedly a caricature both of the biblical position, and of the position that Christians would all profess to hold. Yet few of us would be prepared to deny that, in our worst moments at least (and probably a great deal beyond that), we have so lived as to give countenance to such an accusation.

The trouble is that at heart man always wants his own terms. Long ago the great apostle wrote, 'the natural man receiveth not the things of the Spirit of God: for they are foolishness unto him' (1 Cor. 2: 14). The Christian way as laid down in the New Testament is not obvious. It is not easy for the natural man to take it in even when it is explained to him. Left to ourselves we will do anything rather than accept the truth that in the last resort there is nothing, absolutely nothing, that we can do to merit our salvation. As Emil Brunner remarks, 'all other forms of religion—not to mention philosophy—deal with the problem of guilt apart from the intervention of God, and therefore they come to a "cheap" conclusion. In them man is spared the final humiliation of knowing that the Mediator must bear the punishment instead of him. To this yoke he need not submit. He is not stripped absolutely naked.'[4] But in Christianity he *is* stripped absolutely naked. In the light of the cross it becomes obvious that man's contribution to his own salvation is nil. Christ saves him or he is not saved at all. This is an unpalatable conclusion. No man likes to think that his salvation depends on the sheer mercy of God. Every one of us would prefer to think that we had won our salvation by our own achievement.

The natural man fights desperately to avoid the conclusion that his salvation depends entirely upon the grace of God. In the end he may profess himself religious or irreligious. He may regard himself as a Christian, a humanitarian, an agnostic, a communist, or an atheist. But he will do anything rather than submit to the final humiliation of seeing the whole of his hopes for this world and the next as dependent on the gift of God.

Karl Barth puts it this way, 'transgression of the first commandment inevitably involves that of all others. Sin is always unbelief. And unbelief is always man's faith in

[4] *The Mediator* (London, 1946), p. 474.

himself.'[5] This is a most important point. It reminds us of the scriptural statement that 'sin is lawlessness' (1 Jn. 3: 4, RSV). Sin takes a variety of forms, but basically it is a refusal to submit to God's law. It is a deliberate choosing of man's way rather than God's way. Man cannot take it without putting his trust in himself rather than in God. Thus, whatever form it may take, sin always involves unbelief.

Barth proceeds to connect this up with religion. He goes on immediately, 'and this faith invariably consists in the fact that man makes the mystery of his responsibility his own mystery, instead of accepting it as the mystery of God. It is this faith which is religion. It is contradicted by the revelation attested in the New Testament, which is identical with Jesus Christ as the one who acts for us and on us. This stamps religion a unbelief.'

It is rather startling to have religion equated with unbelief. But if man refuses to accept what Barth calls 'the mystery of God' and prefers to set his own stamp on things, then it is difficult to see how the charge is to be avoided. It is most important to be clear that Christianity places a tremendous emphasis on the wholehearted acceptance of the sovereignty of God. It is God's way that is to be accepted and that in its entirety. Man is not at liberty to impose his pattern on affairs. He may not work out his own ideas, bring them into a superficial harmony with the Bible, and label the result 'Christianity'. If he does, then, whatever he may say, he is acting in unbelief. His very religion is a form of unbelief. If we may cite Jenkins, 'Religion is unbelief also because it is man's attempt to find justification and sanctification for himself on his own terms. This is not the real way to God, but a self-centred way of erecting barriers against him. Our characteristically pious efforts to reconcile God

[5] *Church Dogmatics*, I, *The Doctrine of the Word of God*, Pt. 2 (Edinburgh, 1956), p. 314.

to ourselves must indeed be an abomination in his sight.'[6]

It is interesting that Karl Barth can regard both mysticism and atheism as protests against this false type of religion. This is not to say that he gives firm approval to either. Mysticism may be no more than another variety of human endeavour. The mystic on this view rejects the ordinary religious way because of its inadequacy. But he does not really surrender himself wholeheartedly to God. He simply replaces the conventional religious pattern by his own mystical pattern.

Atheism, he thinks, may at times have something commendable in it. It may represent a deep-seated concern for the right which rejects with decision the false religion. This means, he feels, that we ought to be more respectful to atheism than we always are. Without accepting its presuppositions (or its conclusions) we should nevertheless take heed to ourselves lest we be found practising that false religion which rightly invites its censure. Nevertheless Barth would reject atheism also as being another form of human pride. The atheist like the 'religious' man is setting his own pattern on life. Just as much as the religious man he refuses to submit to the revelation that God has made in Christ.

It will not be surprising after all this to learn that advocates of the views we are considering often contrast religion with faith. Indeed this is a necessity for them. Faith stands for the complete abandonment of self, and of trust in self. Faith is not a superior virtue and merit, but rather a whole-hearted forsaking of all trust in human virtue or merit. It is the attitude which throws itself completely on God. Religion, by contrast, always betokens human effort, as in the case of the mystic or the man of prayer. To all outward appearance these men are giving themselves over to God. But if in actual fact they are refusing to accept God's pattern then their religion must be set in contrast to faith. It does not

[6] *BR*, p. 28.

matter that the pattern they prefer is a religious pattern. If it is not the divine pattern then they are to be censured. It follows from this that Christianity is not to be regarded as simply a better religion than other religions. Religion is always thought of as basically a human creation, 'Christian' religion as well as all others. But true Christianity is not this. The Christian way is to be regarded as superior to other ways not because of any merit or insight in its practitioners or in its system, but only because true Christians are those who have experienced and submitted to the grace of God.

Thus Daniel Jenkins can say, 'The Christian man will see himself as a religious person like anyone else, who has yet been addressed by God and has had his religion overcome by God.'[7] Similarly Barth complains that man 'does not believe'. He goes on to explain, 'If he did, he would listen; but in religion he talks. If he did, he would accept a gift; but in religion he takes something for himself. If he did, he would let God Himself intercede for God: but in religion he ventures to grasp at God. . . . In religion man bolts and bars himself against revelation by providing a substitute, by taking away in advance the very thing which has to be given by God.'[8]

From all this it is plain enough that religion may be the deadly enemy of real Christianity. 'A man's foes shall be they of his own household' (Mt. 10: 36), said our Lord, and the Church has given evidence of the accuracy of the words in every generation. Man loves to manufacture religion. He creates his rites and ceremonies, he works out his way of life, he manufactures a god to his own specifications and does it all in the name of religion. He may be so outwardly pious that he deceives his neighbour. He may be so inwardly convinced that this is right that he deceives himself. Precisely because it is so easy to be religious he walks in this path with alacrity and cheerfully abandons the way of faith.

[7] *BR*, p. 27.　　　　[8] *Op. cit.*, pp. 302 f.

The way of faith is not easy to tread. The fact must be faced that the Church has always found it easier to fulfil her priestly than her prophetic role. The temptation to institutionalism is always with us, and who will profess himself guiltless? We reduce Christianity to the service of an institution, the Church, for this enables us to be active in what is fondly called 'the work of the Lord', while at the same time failing to grapple with the fundamental problem for all Christians, that of winning our generation for Christ. In our little circle of like-minded people we condemn outsiders because they do not come in. Perhaps we even make half-hearted attempts to get them to come in. And then we snuggle down again in the warmth of our fellowship, comforted that we have done all that might reasonably be expected of men in our situation. Fortified with this consolation we concentrate on keeping the institution, the Church, running as it should.

We do well to heed Daniel Jenkins' reminder that, 'The mark of a good church order is not the ease with which its clergy can keep their people in control but the extent of its ability to keep thrusting the church's religion into the crisis of faith and to keep doing this even while it is surrounded by all the precious fruits of faith.'[9] This is no mean task.

It is thus clear enough that there is a sense in which 'religion' is a hindrance to the gospel. It may impede the real work of Christ in the world, and it may help us conceal from ourselves that we are not genuinely living by faith. But now a further question arises. Is there a right religion as well as a wrong one? To this question variant answers are given. The new movement of which we are thinking does not speak with one voice on the matter. Many have the impression that it does, and they are probably helped in this misunderstanding by popular

' BR, p. 46.

presentations like *Honest to God*. But there are wide divergences and to these we now turn.

In the first place let us notice that, though the fiercest and most sustained polemic against 'religion' is surely that of Barth, he is not followed by most recent writers. The trouble apparently is that, after he had rejected all religion that takes its origin in man and man's strivings, Barth proceeded to emphasize the reality and the importance of revelation. This leads to a new kind of 'religion' but it is very definitely religion. But this does not suit the writers of whom we are thinking. Some mention him only to disagree with him. Others, like the Bishop of Woolwich, scarcely refer to him at all. It is curious that a thinker of Barth's stature can be simply ignored. The only one who really takes him seriously is Jenkins, but as we shall see, he is far from typical and in some points seems to part company with the new thought.

Again, few would gather from reading *Honest to God* that Bonhoeffer and Tillich are saying basically different things. Yet they certainly are, as Bonhoeffer himself makes clear. 'Tillich', he says, 'set out to interpret the evolution of the world itself—against its will—in a religious sense, to give it its whole shape through religion. That was very courageous of him, but the world unseated him and went on by itself: he too sought to understand the world better than it understood itself, but it felt entirely *mis*understood, and rejected the imputation. (Of course the world does need to be understood better than it understands itself, but not "religiously" . . .)'.[1]

This ought to be appreciated more widely than it often is. Tillich has some unorthodox ideas about the nature of God, and the Bishop of Woolwich has seized on these. But he is not to be regarded as an upholder of 'religionless Christianity'. He is basically a very religious man, and his system takes religion seriously. Alan Richardson speaks

[1] *Letters*, pp. 108 f.

of Tillich's 'religious atheism',[2] and the phrase is useful, besides arresting. It reminds us that there are peculiarities about his view of God, but that his concern for 'religion' should not be called in question.

The movement against religion seems to have received its impetus from Barth. We have already seen some of the things he says. He was at first associated with others such as Tillich, Thurneysen, and Brunner, but his massive attack on 'religion' affected his associates in different ways. Bonhoeffer felt that Barth had started off in the right way but that he did not go far enough. 'Barth was the first theologian to begin the criticism of religion,— and that remains his really great merit—but he set in its place the positivist doctrine of revelation which says in effect, "Take it or leave it"';[3] 'he gave no concrete guidance, either in dogmatics or in ethics, on the non-religious interpretation of theological concepts. There lies his limitation. . . .'[4] For Bonhoeffer the non-religious approach is all-important. Barth is welcomed to the extent to which he set it forward, and blamed to the extent to which he failed to go through with it.

But with Tillich it is different. He did not see Barth as having opened up a promising new line of thinking which could be taken further. He reacted against much in Barth, and specifically against the non-religious idea. It will perhaps help if we quote James Richmond's summary: 'We turn now to Tillich's sharp deviation from the extreme religionless doctrine of man of the Barthian school. Tillich's image of man (and this may come as a salutary shock to those who are by now accustomed to hearing Tillich and Bonhoeffer bracketed together!) bears

[2] *Four Anchors*, p. 6. 'The religious atheism of Tillich is un-interesting because it is impossible to confute. One cannot pick a quarrel with the Ground of Being; but, then, one cannot go to the stake for it either.'
[3] *Letters*, p. 95.
[4] *Letters*, p. 109.

little resemblance to Bonhoeffer's. Tillich has reacted violently against Barthianism, and his polemic against its doctrine of man has been fierce. He accuses it of teaching that God's revelation must be thrown at religionless man like a stone. He has even charged it with heresy; it is *docetic* and *monophysite* in its devaluation of man. It is irrational, because it holds, quite senselessly, that man could receive an answer to a question which a religionless man could not possibly ask! Tillich has demanded that theology should go beyond the Dialectical (and that means Bonhoeffer's) position.

'Tillich interprets man in a "religious" way. Tillichian man decidedly has a "God-shaped blank" in his soul; a religious *a priori* assuredly exists. Tillich believes firmly in *homo religiosus,* who is not come of age in Bonhoeffer's sense, but is very much afraid of the dark. Man cannot escape God, because his awareness is constantly invaded by despair, finitude, guilt, suffering, loneliness, estrangement, doubt and meaninglessness. These factors throw man beyond themselves to God, Being-itself, who is beyond the inescapable tension between man as he ought to be and man as he is. Man is essentially religious, because awareness of his finitude, for example, drives him towards the infinite by whom and for whom he was created. What a sharp contrast between Tillichian man and the religionless man of the extreme Barthians!'[5]

As a matter of fact this aspect of Tillich's thought is plain enough even in passages which are quoted in *Honest to God* (though attention is not drawn to the fact). Thus Dr. Robinson quotes Tillich as saying, 'The state of our whole life is estrangement from others and ourselves, because we are estranged from the Ground of our being';[6] 'We always remain in the power of that from which we are estranged. That fact brings us to the ulti-

[5] *Four Anchors,* pp. 41 f.
[6] *HTG,* p. 79.

mate depth of sin: separated and yet bound, estranged and yet belonging, destroyed and yet preserved, the state which is called despair';[7] 'Grace strikes us when we are in great pain and restlessness. It strikes us when we walk through the dark valley of a meaningless and empty life.'[8] It is surprising that Dr. Robinson never grapples with the view of religion and of man's need which is expressed in such passages. And they could be multiplied many times, as even a cursory acquaintance with Tillich's writings makes clear. Tillich has some unusual views about the nature of God, but he ought never to be cited in favour of 'religionless Christianity'.

It would not be difficult to show similarly that Bonhoeffer differs sharply from Bultmann. As with Barth, he thinks that Bultmann began well (in his demythologizing) but did not go far enough. Bultmann was ready to abandon the miracles, the ascension and the like, but he retained fundamentally religious conceptions. 'You cannot, as Bultmann imagines, separate God and miracles, but you do have to be able to interpret and proclaim *both* of them in a "non-religious" sense. Bultman's approach is really at bottom the liberal one (i.e. abridging the Gospel), whereas I seek to think theologically.'[9] Some of Bultmann's approach Bonhoeffer found acceptable. But it would not be right to class them together, as Bonhoeffer himself recognizes.

It is important for us to be clear that not all the writers who are popularly lumped together are really trying to say the same thing. There are differences, and these not in unimportant, peripheral matters, but at the very heart of their understanding of theology. In other words, those who oppose the advocates of 'religionless Christianity' are not faced with a monolithic phalanx, but with a series of individuals who have no strong link

[7] *HTG*, pp. 79 f.
[8] *HTG*, p. 81.
[9] *Letters*, p. 94; see also p. 110.

between them and some of whom are engaged eagerly against one another.[1]

We should also be quite clear that, where these theologians, or some of them, are agreed, what is in question is not a minor change here and there in things not regarded as of crucial importance in orthodox religion. The movement is radical and looks for radical changes. Thus David L. Edwards speaks of Christians who 'are quite ready for a wholesale revision of the Church's doctrine and customs, worship and work, organization and architecture, morals and politics, and are ready to declare themselves in favour of change even when they do not see exactly where the process of change will end'.[2] This will seem to some to be welcome evidence of a spirit of adventure. There is a refusal to be hide-bound, a readiness to go wherever the Spirit of God leads.

To others it will appear to be no more than sheer irresponsibility, for what is at stake is not a few private ideas and practices but the future of the very Church of God. They will feel no less constrained to follow the leading of the Spirit of God than their unorthodox opposite numbers, but they will bear in mind that there is such a thing as 'the spirit of error' as well as 'the Spirit of truth'. They will want some clear indication that when they are asked to renounce beliefs and practices the request is made for good reason. They will want to know, at least in general terms, where these changes lead, for they feel that they have no right to throw away a birth-right that has been handed on to them from past generations. With David Edwards they recognize 'the danger

---

[1] There are differences also in important doctrines which do not concern us directly here, as when R. Gregor Smith finds it hard to see how Bonhoeffer could ever 'have constructed an orthodox doctrine of the relation of Christ to the Father' from the views contained in the letters (*The New Man*, London, 1956, p. 103).

[2] *HTGD*, p. 21.

that the faithful will be misled by their own accredited teachers, because these teachers, without being honest enough to say so explicitly, will by implication abandon the essential faith in God through Christ'.[3]

I rather wonder whether all those who clamber on the 'religionless' band-waggon quite understand where it is going and what it is. Thus Theodore O. Wedel points out that 'A broken spindle or a defective computer are not mended by prayer'. And of the workaday world he says, 'We have to act and to make decisions in that world "as if God did not exist", but the decisions are nevertheless *before* God.'[4] Unless this is carefully understood it is not what Bonhoeffer is saying at all. He is not simply affirming that there is a right place for religion and that this is not in the sphere of the secular. He is not saying merely that there are certain principles which operate in secular life and these not religious. He is arguing for '*religionless*' life. If words have meaning he is saying that we have no right to assume that men ought to be 'religious' in any part of their life. Men 'come of age' have no need of that attitude.

Similarly to Wedel, Daniel Jenkins thinks of religion as 'man's search for God on man's own terms, as his effort to make some kind of adjustment to the "ground of being" on a level less radical than that of the self-forgetful commitment of faith'.[5] If what Wedel and Jenkins understand by 'religion' were all that is in question it is difficult to see what all the fuss is about. Whatever their defects in practice, all Christians would surely agree that there is a proper place for the secular and that man must not search for God on his own terms so that he can avoid the total commitment of faith. That

[3] *HTGD*, p. 30. *Cf.* the woman who wrote that 'revolution apart, Christian faith and practice must ultimately be abandoned' (*HTGD*, p. 72), and who saw *Honest to God* as expressing the same view.

[4] *HTGD*, p. 185.

[5] *HTGD*, p. 210.

is common ground for all orthodox Christians. The difficulty with Bonhoeffer is that he is not pleading for the doing away of a false religion, but for the doing away of religion. His demand is far more radical than some of his followers have yet realized. And it is the radical nature of his demand that proves a stumbling-block for orthodox believers. 'God is teaching us that we must live as men who can get along very well without him,'[6] writes Bonhoeffer. This does not mean that 'religion' must be kept in its place. It means that there is no place for 'religion'.

F. Gerald Downing seems to have understood Bonhoeffer better than many who invoke him. He points out in his article, 'Man's Coming of Age',[7] that Bonhoeffer differs from Jenkins,[8] Barth, Heaton, Bultmann, Vidler and others. All these in one way or another find a place for a purified religion. Bonhoeffer does not. 'Bonhoeffer really did query the rightness of trying to maintain in this century *any sort of religion at all.* Words, theological or pious; a concern for men's "inner life", for conscience, for "religious consciousness", for "the individual"; the place of the Church, parish, preaching, *cultus,* Christian devotional life, all are questioned, all seen as probably ephemeral, disposable. Certainly all need a radically secular re-interpretation.'[9]

A little later Downing points us to the kind of thing that presented a problem for Bonhoeffer. 'He finds strong, and often good, non-religious people; often kind and self-surrendering; people who have lived life fully. What are they? Devils in the guise of angels of light? *Homines naturaliter Christiani*? Christians by their own efforts? Or are they just possibly men being redeemed

[6] *Letters,* p. 122.
[7] *Prism,* Dec. 1962, pp. 31–42.
[8] An editorial in *Prism,* Sept. 1962, pp. 1–4, characterizes Jenkins' book as 'dangerous' because it misunderstands Bonhoeffer and finds a place for a purified religion.
[9] *Op. cit.,* pp. 33 f. (Downing's italics).

through the death and resurrection of Christ who is God of History? And if God can produce such men as these without religion what part could he have beside for religion in their lives? If he can elicit such obedience from them what further cultic response could he want or obtain?'[1]

Bonhoeffer does not express it in just these terms in the *Letters*, but Downing does seem to reflect faithfully one aspect of his thought. Bonhoeffer consistently deprecates any attempt to convict of sin men who belong to a world 'come of age'. He can say that for theology, 'God thus became the answer to life's problems, the solution of its distresses and conflicts. As a result, if anyone had no such difficulties, if he refused to identify himself in sympathy with those who had, it was no good trying to win him for God. The only way of getting at him was to show that he had all these problems, needs and conflicts without being aware of it or owning up to it . . . this is the attitude I am contending against. When Jesus blessed sinners, they were real sinners, but Jesus did not make every man a sinner first. . . . Never did Jesus throw any doubt on a man's health, vigour or fortune, regarded in themselves, or look upon them as evil fruits.'[2] In line with this he speaks approvingly of the man who 'has neither time nor inclination for thinking about his intellectual despair and regarding his modest share of happiness as a trial, a trouble or a disaster'.[3] Similarly he complains of 'the "priestly" snuffing around in the sins of men in order to catch them out. It is as though a beautiful house could only be known after a cobweb had been found in the furthermost corner of the cellar'.[4] It is in this spirit that he deprecates the attempt to see Goethe and Napoleon as sinners merely because they were not faithful husbands.[5]

The same attitude underlies Bonhoeffer's setting out

---

[1] *Op. cit.*, p. 35.   [2] *Letters*, pp. 114 f.
[3] *Letters*, p. 108.   [4] *Letters*, p. 117.   [5] *Letters*, p. 118.

of his positive understanding of the 'religionless' way. As we have already noticed, he says that 'God is teaching us that we must live as men who can get along very well without him'.[6] In line with this, man 'must therefore plunge himself into the life of a godless world, without attempting to gloss over its ungodliness with a veneer of religion or trying to transfigure it. He must live a "Worldly" life and so participate in the suffering of God'.[7] To be 'godless' may well be a virtue. 'Now that it has come of age, the world is more godless, and perhaps it is for that very reason nearer to God than ever before.'[8]

Sometimes people feel a difficulty with this aspect of Bonhoeffer's thought because they remember so well his *The Cost of Discipleship,* and this new way looks suspiciously like one form of what he then castigated as 'cheap grace'. Probably we should not try to set the two into too sharp an antithesis, but it is the case that he had second thoughts about *The Cost of Discipleship.* Thus he says, 'I thought I could acquire faith by trying to live a holy life, or something like it. It was in this phase that I wrote *The Cost of Discipleship.* To-day I can see the dangers of this book, though I am prepared to stand by what I wrote. Later I discovered and am still discovering up to this very moment that it is only by living completely in this world that one learns to believe.'[9]

It is important to be clear on the very radical nature of 'religionless Christianity' as Bonhoeffer advocates it. He is not pleading, as some of his followers apparently think, for a new type of religion, purged of its errors, adult, mature, alert to face the needs of the day. He is saying that for some people at any rate, those who manifest the right qualities of life, no religion at all is necessary. God has evidently brought them into this kind of life. The Church cannot presume now to lay other demands on them, asking that they become religious.

[6] *Letters*, p. 122.   [7] *Letters*, pp. 122 f.
[8] *Letters*, p. 124.   [9] *Letters*, p. 125.

It is possible that Bonhoeffer envisaged some men as continuing to be religious. Downing maintains that this is the case with himself. 'For the time being, I have myself to stay religious. I know no other way. I must share in the Eucharist, offer to God some token praise that I intend entirely for him, and not for him through his world. I am religious.'[1] But he sees this as no reason for asking others to be 'religious'. And notice his, 'For the time being'. Religionless Christianity in the form in which Bonhoeffer and Downing understand it means what it says. Man not yet come of age may need religion. But man come of age does not.

Bonhoeffer is emphatic about this. He can say, 'The time when men could be told everything by means of words, whether theological or simply pious, is over, and so is the time of inwardness and conscience, which is to say the time of religion as such. We are proceeding towards a time of no religion at all: men as they are now simply cannot be religious any more.' A little later he says, 'Our whole nineteen-hundred-year-old Christian preaching and theology rests upon "the religious premise" of man. . . . But if one day it becomes apparent that this *a priori* "premise" simply does not exist, but was a historical and temporary form of human self-expression, i.e. if we reach the stage of being radically without religion . . . what does that mean for "Christianity"? It means that the linchpin is removed from the whole structure of our Christianity to date.'[2]

The extreme radicalism of Bonhoeffer's demand should not be missed. So radical is he that some of those who invoke his name have watered down his words, apparently thinking that he could not possibly have meant what he said. But he seems to me to have been in dead earnest. It is writers such as Downing who have correctly understood him. He is not calling for a vigorous reform of religion. He is looking for a time of no religion. We

[1] *Op. cit.,* p. 41.   [2] *Letters,* p. 91.

can agree with him or disagree with him. But we should refrain from the temptation to rewrite him.

This seems to me to be what some of his defenders are doing. Thus Martin E. Marty never gets to grips with this aspect of Bonhoeffer's thought. He complains of 'superficial dismissal by his critics';[3] he says that Bonhoeffer 'did not mean an uncritical baptism of the unredeemed world!';[4] he dismisses 'the secularist interpretations (in many American student groups)';[5] he thinks it misinterpretation that Bonhoeffer taught 'a direct and uncritical acceptance of the world';[6] he thinks it superficial 'to abandon the disciplined devotional life in the name of religionless Christianity'.[7] He and his collaborators bring forward a good deal of evidence to show that Bonhoeffer was a profoundly religious man and that he based his theology on certain great Christian truths. But they do this by quoting largely from his earlier works, and even selectively from the *Letters*.

What they do not do is to grapple with the key passages for 'religionless Christianity' in the *Letters* and show that their contentions are true of these passages. I am not concerned to maintain that Bonhoeffer everywhere taught secularism. That is obviously false. It is only in certain passages in the *Letters* that he teaches 'religionless Christianity'. The idea must stand or fall with these passages, not with the whole of Bonhoeffer's writings. My contention is that his thought was not unified. I am not concerned here with his other ideas, but only with 'religionless Christianity'. And the truth is that the position of Marty and other defenders of Bonhoeffer is that they are not doing justice to what he *said* about 'religionless Christianity'. They are assuring us that they know what he *meant* and making this something other than his words.

[3] *The place of Bonhoeffer* (London, 1963), p. 16.
[4] *Op. cit.*, p. 19.   [5] *Op. cit.*, p. 26.
[6] *Op. cit.*, p. 144.   [7] *Op. cit.*, p. 167.

Walter Harrelson recognizes the self-contradictory nature of Bonhoeffer's thought. He says, 'I find here a kind of dualism in Bonhoeffer's program. He wants to find a way to present Christian faith by means of non-religious equivalents of such terms as repentance, faith, justification, rebirth, sanctification. But he also wants the Church to live a secret life in which the mystery of Word and Sacrament is secured from profanation. The Church, on this view, lives two lives—one public and the other private. This dualism is far more dangerous, in my view, than the "positivism of revelation" of Barth (if that view of Barth be accepted) or the "not far enough" of Bultmann.'[8]

Whatever be the truth of Harrelson's estimates of the relative merits of the positions of Bonhoeffer, Barth and Bultmann, it ought to be clearly recognized that these positions *are* different. We are faced not with slight variants on a basically similar theme, but with basically different positions. If we accept Bonhoeffer then we must reject Barth and Bultmann. If we accept Barth we must reject Bultmann and Bonhoeffer. If we accept Bultmann it is hard to see how we can do other than reject Bonhoeffer and Barth.

Paul van Buren is sometimes cited as belonging to this new movement,[9] so perhaps it is worth pointing out that his position is not that of the others. He is interested in expressing Christianity in secular terms and he can speak of the Christian, 'himself a secular man, who realizes that the juxtaposition of his faith, expressed in traditional terms, and his ordinary way of thinking, causes a spiritual schizophrenia'.[1] But he rejects firmly the 'religionless' approach. 'Many theologians say that one of the major difficulties confronting the Christian who is himself a secular man lies in the nature of religion

[8] M. E. Marty, *op. cit.*, p. 136.
[9] *E.g.* by the Bishop of Woolwich, *HTGD*, p. 242.
[1] *The Secular Meaning of the Gospel* (London, 1963), p. 77.

and the confusion between religion and Christian faith.
We have argued that the difficulty lies rather in the
character of the language of faith, that the problem is not
so much one of bad religion as it is one of bad, or at
least unworkable, language.'[2] This is impossible to square
with Bonhoeffer's 'religionless Christianity', and, indeed,
shortly afterwards van Buren explicitly repudiates
Bonhoeffer's view.[3] For good measure, he also finds
Bultmann and Ogden wanting.[4]

I have been at pains to point out that there are differences among those who advocate religionless Christianity. Some of them do look for a right religion. But
the logic of the position is with Bonhoeffer. We should
be quite clear that his demand was radical. We have to
face the question whether this is in line with the mind
of Christ, or whether it is another form of man's perennial self-sufficiency.

[2] *Op. cit.*, p. 81.

[3] *Op. cit.*, p. 84. Later he says that his method 'is one which
never occurred to Bonhoeffer' (*op. cit.*, p. 171).

[4] *Op. cit.*, p. 100. It is also worth noticing, though it is not our
immediate concern, that van Buren rejects the view of Tillich
and Robinson that instead of 'God' we should speak of 'our
ultimate concern', *etc.* (*op. cit.*, p. 170).

CHAPTER TWO

THE GOD OF THE GAPS

A MAJOR concern of the theologians of whom we are thinking is that God must be seen as the God of all life. They constantly register their protest against thinking of Him as concerned only with a segment or segments of life. We shall return to this point in other connections. Here we are concerned to note their protest against regarding God as a convenient means of explaining gaps in our knowledge of the world and of life.

Notably is this the case in the realm of scientific discovery. When the modern scientific movement began to get under way, and certain scientists appeared to be so proud of their achievements and of their knowledge that they found no place for God, the tactic adopted by some Christians was to emphasize the gaps in human knowledge. 'Man knows so very little,' they reasoned. 'We must think of God as the only adequate explanation of the mysteries of the universe.'

It soon became apparent, however, that there is a major drawback to this defence. The sphere assigned to God (and hence the importance of God) progressively shrinks. The theologian proclaims, perhaps, that there is mystery in the commonest of things. No man, he may once have said, knows how that common and necessary fluid, water, is made up. Does the scientist come to discover that water is composed of two elements, hydrogen and oxygen? The theologian counters that there is still mystery. God knows, though the scientist does not, of what hydrogen and oxygen are composed. Then the scientist discovers that the atoms of hydrogen and oxygen are composed of protons and electrons. The theologian is no whit disconcerted. He now maintains that though the scientist knows something of the way atoms are composed he does not know what protons and electrons are. And so the chase goes on.

Once God is seen in this way filling in the gaps in scientific knowledge, the theologian is necessarily engaged in a process of continual retreat. Every new discovery squeezes God a little further out of His universe. When we consider the mighty strides made by scientific discovery in recent years we can see that this particular theological procedure is exceedingly hazardous, to say the least of it.

In similar fashion men are extending the area of knowledge in realms other than the scientific. Where in earlier days the theologian used to fall back on the comforting thought that the things that man does not know God knows, the things man cannot do God can do, his opposite number in all sorts of disciplines has developed a disconcerting knack of coming up with perfectly feasible explanations on the human or natural level. There is less and less need, accordingly, for the seeker after knowledge to think about the place of God. And the uncomfortable thought rises persistently in our minds that there is something wrong with a God who is so continually on the retreat. It is scarcely possible for the student to do other than give up belief in such a God. His intellectual integrity forbids him to do anything else.

Dietrich Bonhoeffer puts the case this way: 'I will try to define my position from the historical angle. The movement beginning about the thirteenth century (I am not going to get involved in any arguments about the exact date) towards the autonomy of man (under which head I place the discovery of the laws by which the world lives and manages in science, social and political affairs, art, ethics and religion) has in our time reached a certain completion. Man has learned to cope with all questions of importance without recourse to God as a working hypothesis. In questions concerning science, art, and even ethics, this has become an understood thing which one scarcely dares to tilt at any more. But for the last hundred years or so it has been increasingly true of religious questions also: it is becoming evident that everything gets along without "God", and just as well as before. As in the scientific field, so in human affairs generally, what we call "God" is being more and more edged out of life, losing more and more ground.'[1]

This protest has relevance even though no self-respecting Christian apologist these days would ever set forth a view of God which regards Him in this way as a God of the gaps only. Yet there is a call to us to give heed to the implications of our method. It is easy enough to adopt all unconsciously a manner of commending the faith which in the end reduces to just another way of putting God into the gaps. R. Gregor Smith sees recent history this way: 'Before the advancing battalions of intelligence and reason and scepticism, as one area of knowledge after another was captured for technology, or science, or psychology, God has been rescued by too willing hands. The children of light have been happily engaged in drawing God back into the darkness, beyond the frontiers of assured life, into the region which is euphemistically called the mystery of God. The mystery of God has been equated with a kind of *terra incognita*, an as-yet unknowable rather than as a truly ineffable mystery, which is to say a *present* mystery whose mystery is an actual, encountered, lived experience of an incomprehensible but not inapprehensible gift.'[2] This kind of defence of theism is deplorable. God is not to be known by reason of the gaps in human knowledge, and we render a disservice to Christianity when we speak as though He were.

The accusation that the Church has made God into a

[1] *Letters,* pp. 106 f.
[2] *The New Man* (London, 1956), p. 99.

'God of the gaps' is perhaps more relevant to the practical living out of life than to the theological explanation we give of it. It certainly is true that in the ordinary affairs of Christian living some of those who espouse the name of Christ have been guilty of acting as though there are certain matters which are well within the competence of man. These matters scarcely need praying about, and we need not concern ourselves as though God were in them. We simply go ahead and do them. But there are other matters which are beyond our powers. Confronted with these we give ourselves fervently to prayer and we look to God to enable us to win through. The logical outcome of this is that when our technique for handling situations improves a little there is correspondingly less for God to do. This represents a process whereby the religious man progressively squeezes his God out of life.

This whole attitude must be emphatically repudiated. God is in all of life. There is no department of living, no matter how familiar with it we feel, from which God is absent. All that we do we do in God, and with God's help.

Sometimes Bonhoeffer puts this in a way which cannot but gain wide acceptance. 'One must abandon every attempt to make something of oneself,' he says, 'whether it be a saint, a converted sinner, a churchman (the priestly type, so-called!), a righteous man or an unrighteous one, a sick man or a healthy one. This is what I mean by worldliness—taking life in one's stride, with all its duties and problems, its successes and failures, its experiences and helplessness. It is in such a life that we throw ourselves utterly into the arms of God and participate in his sufferings in the world and watch with Christ in Gethsemane.'[3] This is not quite the way I would put it. For one thing it says too little about our dependence on the Holy Spirit if we are to live out the Christian life. But in its whole-hearted affirmation of the need for the

[3] *Letters*, p. 125.

Christian to get into the business of living life to the full it is saying something which must be of concern to all biblically minded Christians.

Sometimes there have been movements in the Church which recognize our tendency to fragment life. Those who proclaimed the 'social gospel' may serve as an example. They were concerned for society, and therefore they protested against a form of Christianity that saw God as interested in less than the whole human situation. We may well feel that they tried to make things too simple. The criticism has been made, rightly in my opinion, that the movement as a whole had inadequate views about human sinfulness, and that it was not true to New Testament teaching about the kingdom of God. In its concern for social questions it seems to have overlooked other aspects of the gospel. It substituted one unbalanced interpretation of Christianity for another. But its very existence was a protest against a form of Christianity which saw God as concerned with too small a segment of life.

And the new movement we are considering is, in one aspect, a further protest against the same thing. As Christians we must be perpetually on our guard lest we unwittingly take up a position which gives the outsider the impression that, while recognizing fully the autonomy of modern man in certain areas of life, we bring God in as a convenient explanation of things of which we are ignorant in the realm beyond that. Whenever we give such an impression, however pure our motives, we are in fact directing man along the way that in the end leads inevitably to atheism.

At the same time it should be noticed that this criticism is not one which is rightly to be levied at the orthodox only. Though they do not notice it, there is much in the new position which can lead to the same conclusion. In the present study we are concerned with 'religionless Christianity' and not with the whole of the position taken up in such a book as *Honest to God*. Thus we do not discuss here the view of the nature of God characteristic of the group of modern writers of whom we are thinking. But we must now notice, if only briefly, their view that God is to be thought of as 'the ground of our being', as 'ultimate reality', or the like. He is not apparently regarded as a Person. That belongs to the outmoded thinking they are seeking to replace. It is not easy to see what 'ground of our being' or 'ultimate reality' means unless 'that ultimate dimension of nature and existence inexplicable by naturalistic thought-processes'.[4] James Richmond points out that even the agnostic or the humanist can agree on 'a "religious" attitude towards the unplumbed depths of existence', and he goes on, 'Without faith in some such depths scientific research would perish. But such depths are not something "other than" or "beyond" nature, but that important aspect of it, the object of scientific faith, which engenders and nourishes the scientific attitude. In short, they are those *as yet* unrealized values and unexplored depths whose existence spurs on scientific research. . . . To confuse these depths with the God of the Hebrew Bible would be a vast theological error. And to invite humanists to reject millennia-old conceptions of God in favour of "depths" understood in these terms would be to invite the conclusion that theology is little other than playing with words, or that it is again using the technique condemned by Bonhoeffer of locating God in the gaps of our understanding.'[5]

Of course it may be possible to understand 'the ground of our being' in a way which does not come under this condemnation. Until the expression is defined much more closely than it is at present we cannot altogether rule out this possibility. But we can say that at present there is no sign of it. The concept does appear to be a way of

---

[4] *Four Anchors*, p. 45.
[5] *Loc. cit.*

referring to the 'ultimate dimension of nature and existence', and thus to be the proper object of scientific research.

In all this I am not suggesting that, because there is a flaw in the way the newer theologians are writing, we therefore need not take seriously the accusations they make against traditional ways of thinking. I have already pointed out that it is all too easy to fall into this error, and it is well that orthodox Christians give heed to the warning given. But while we take heed to the mote which is alleged to be in our eye, others might well look to the saying about a beam.

To conclude. One of the accusations made with the greatest confidence is that orthodox Christianity has been too ready to see God only in the gaps in human knowledge. To the extent to which this is true we are challenged to repent and to gain a broader vision of God's activity. God is in all of life. We must think and live as those who are sure of this.

way of coping with the situations that arose in those
areas. This opened up the way to superstitious practices
of many kinds. It also left men feeling helpless in many
situations.

But in more recent times that is all changed. Advances
in knowledge have given man power . . .

CHAPTER THREE

THE WORLD'S 'COMING OF AGE'

CHAPTER THREE

THE WORLD'S 'COMING OF AGE'

ONE of the catchphrases greatly used in writings
of the type of which we are thinking is that the
world has 'come of age'. Since this is a very
important concept it behoves us to give serious attention
to it. First, let us notice how Bonhoeffer speaks of it:
'Catholic and Protestant historians are agreed that it is
in this development' (*i.e.* the development mentioned in
the quotation on pp. 31 f. above) 'that the great defection
from God, from Christ, is to be discerned, and the more
they bring in and make use of God and Christ in opposition to this trend, the more the trend itself considers
itself to be anti-Christian. The world which has attained
to a realization of itself and of the laws which govern its
existence is so sure of itself that we become frightened.
False starts and failures do not make the world deviate
from the path and development it is following; they are
accepted with fortitude and detachment as part of the
bargain, and even an event like the present war is no
exception. Christian apologetic has taken the most varying forms of opposition to this self-assurance. Efforts are
made to prove to a world thus come of age that it cannot
live without the tutelage of "God".'[1]

Bonhoeffer is greatly concerned that men should not
be compelled to go back on their own history. Through
the centuries they have come to know a great deal more
about the world and how they should live in it and this
should now govern them. They should live on the basis
of what they have come to know, and not on the basis of
irrational religious taboos. In earlier ages, many areas of
life were regarded as dominated by God. Man had no

[1] *Letters*, p. 107.

way of coping with the situations that arose in those areas. This opened up the way to superstitious practices of many kinds. It also left men feeling helpless in many situations.

But in more recent times that is all changed. Advances in psychology have given man a greater knowledge of himself and his own thought-processes. Advances in science and technology have increased his power to effect his will and to produce the kind of things that his modern civilization demands. Advances in ethics, sociology and the rest have made man more sure of himself. He is no longer troubled as he was in an earlier day by his own inadequacy. He has come of age.

Perhaps the best and most positive understanding of this is in terms of freedom. Daniel Jenkins can say: 'Modern men have "come of age" in the sense that they recognize that they are no longer under tutors nor under the control of the rulers of this world but are called to freedom and responsibility. They do not need religion in the limited sense which Bonhoeffer means when he speaks of it, nor are they able to live for long on the basis of dictatorship about how they should behave by institutions for which they hold uncritical reverence. They are compelled now to live with their freedom. . . . The coming of age of man means that he cannot live any more with the gods. He can only find the fulfilment of his freedom in bondservice of Christ or drive himself to destruction with ever-increasing speed.'[2]

This is a fact and we must face it. Man has outgrown many earlier attitudes. Man's knowledge and man's power have enlarged. There is something almost impious

[2] *BR*, p. 85. Similarly R. Gregor Smith says, man 'saw himself as free, and as responsible for making his own life, and as open to a future which was not an arbitrary or threatening disposition of fate, but was awaiting him as his own destiny. History came to be seen as the way in which man understood his own being as the free and responsible climax to his given situation' (*The New Man*, London, 1956, p. 41).

in the suggestion that he should renounce his knowledge
and forgo the use of his powers. He is called upon to
make the fullest use of both. He must live with his freedom. He is not subject any longer to the taboos, superstitions, and limitations of earlier ages. As Jenkins puts
it in the passage just quoted, 'he cannot live any more
with the gods.' There is no reason why he should.

All this must be granted. Nevertheless it is more than
doubtful whether 'come of age' is a particularly good
description of the modern world. As used by many it
seems to have about it the implication that in all previous
ages man was but a child, whereas now he is fully grown
up. He is a responsible, reasoning adult. He is emanci-
pated. He has the key of the door.

It is this way of understanding 'coming of age' which
is at fault. It is true that man has developed through the
centuries, and that at some points he is now more
advanced by far than in earlier days. But only at some
points. In many areas of life modern man is at best no
more advanced than, and at worst far behind, the men of
earlier generations. Few, for example, would be found
to maintain that our philosophers have advanced significantly beyond Plato, or our wise men beyond Socrates,
or our thinkers beyond the men of the Renaissance, or
our men of art beyond the medieval artists (or those of
ancient Greece for that matter). Few would claim that
this age is outstanding for its production of great art or
great literature. And, when full allowance has been made
for altruistic movements on an international scale as seen
in the Red Cross or the humanitarian activities of the
United Nations Organization or the like, it can scarcely
be claimed that in recent years man has attained great
heights morally.

In some respects this is a most callous and unen-
lightened age. We should not forget that it is modern
man who has designed and used the atom bomb. Though
he has great facilities for production and distribution it

is modern man who acquiesces in a situation where some of the world's population have more than enough of this world's goods so that they live in affluence, while others go to bed hungry every night. There is a constant and bloody carnage on our roads, though few of us have any conscience about it. The prevalence of psychoses and neuroses in modern man makes depressing reading, as does the growth of juvenile delinquency. Our attitude to the colour bar, our shameless exploitation of sex, our ready tolerance of the miseries necessarily attendant on the way drink and gambling are used in our communities are other examples.

There is much to support A. Leonard Griffith when he says, 'I prefer General Omar Bradley's phrase about "nuclear giants and ethical infants", which compares man to an 18-month-old child who has suddenly achieved physical and mental proportions of adulthood but in his attitude and behaviour still acts like a helpless baby. A civilization that spends billions to put a man on the moon and simultaneously sponsors a tear-jerking "Freedom from Hunger Week" is hardly a civilization come of age, capable of finding within itself the means of its own salvation.'[3]

These words should be carefully weighed. There is no call for us to depreciate the very real values of modern life and culture. But we ought not to be so hypnotized by man's recent achievement in certain areas of life that we are blind to his failures and shortcomings in others. In particular we have to overlook a great deal in the tensions and insecurities of life for many modern Western men if we are to hold that our civilization has within itself the resources to work out its salvation. It makes a high-sounding phrase for Bonhoeffer to talk about men as 'come of age'. But it does not accord with the facts.[4]

---

[3] *HTGD*, p. 103.
[4] Dr. Robinson now says that the expression has been misunderstood, and adds, 'I should be perfectly prepared to accept

Notice also how self-centred we are when we use the phrase. We conveniently overlook the fact that the affluent Western communities are a minority. Most of the world today is poor and hungry and illiterate. It lacks adequate sanitation and medical facilities. It looks and longs for education. It is both politically minded and politically naïve. It longs for freedom and all too often has to live under a dictatorship. It is angry and restless and always calling for a better life. It is more interested in full bellies than in well-stocked minds. Has it really come of age?

Even in our Western communities things are not exactly rosy. We should not forget that the civilization which could produce a Bonhoeffer could produce also a Hitler. Beside the tremendous achievements of German science and German culture generally we must set Auschwitz and Belsen. America and England can both recall riots connected with colour. The miserable story could be prolonged. It is difficult to find any area of life, science and technology apart, in which this age may fairly claim to excel; and even there the achievement is confined to a comparatively small proportion of the world's population. In other departments of life we show no great superiority over earlier ages. We are no more 'of age' than they.

Sometimes writers of the school of which we are thinking recognize this. Thus A. R. Vidler wishes to 'distinguish between what has been happening to educated and sensitive minds, to the intellectually and emotionally mature, on the one hand, and the persistence and recrudescence of infantile passions and superstitions

in its place the notion that man has reached adolescence' (*HTGD*, p. 270, n. 3). It is to be doubted if he has really come to grips even now with the force of the criticism offered. Outside a very few people in a very restricted area of life there is no real evidence for growth of this sort. Even adolescence is scarcely a happy description of the modern world, and Omar Bradley's phrase may be nearer the mark.

in contemporary societies, on the other'. This is an important concession. It indicates that not all can be said to have come of age, but only 'educated and sensitive minds, the intellectually and emotionally mature'. Moreover Vidler goes on, 'Who indeed will venture to claim that he has wholly attained to intellectual or emotional maturity? It is to be hoped that the present state of the world is not a register of man's coming of age.'[5] If such a man as Dr. Vidler dares not claim to have 'come of age' in this sense, one wonders who has. Obviously only the tiniest of minorities can claim to be numbered among this élite. And this raises the question whether there is any point in using of the modern world in general a concept which applies only to a small handful of the educated and sensitive.

Perhaps this is the place to notice the extraordinary silence preserved by the writers of whom we are thinking on the whole subject of the Person and work of the Holy Spirit. I do not mean that they never mention Him. They do occasionally. And some of them mention Him more than occasionally when they are not dealing with 'religionless Christianity'. But when this new way is being expounded no real place is found for the Spirit of the living God. This is an astounding omission. When we think of the place given the Spirit in the New Testament it is plain enough that any movement which fails to give an important place to the Holy Spirit is self-condemned. 'Religionless Christianity' is not at all happy with the idea that man come of age needs divine help. Its neglect of the Holy Spirit is a further example of its fundamental man-centredness.

It is moreover true to say that most of those who use the 'coming of age' terminology do so partly at least with a view to explaining the modern disregard of organized religion. The idea is that in medieval times man, still in his infancy, was necessarily subject to the tutelage of the

[5] *Soundings*, p. 253.

Church. But now he has grown up. He is independent and free. He sees no need of being in subjection to the Church. So he breaks out into secularism. Secularism is thus seen, in part at any rate, as a protest against an earlier clericalism. There is a large element of good in it. It represents a development which is not only natural but right. Man come of age *ought* to see that the Church has exceeded its powers in laying hold of him. He *ought* to live unshackled by the practices and beliefs of traditionally-minded Christians.

But, as we have seen, this is not an accurate picture of modern man. He has not really 'come of age' in this sense at all. It is simply not in accord with the facts to regard modern man as though he had seriously considered the claims of the Church, seen that they were incompatible with advances made in all departments of life, and therefore rejected them. On the contrary, he has never even thought about them. Your average secular modern man could not give a reasonable account of what the Church believes if he tried. He has rejected what he has never troubled to understand. 'His situation is not that he has achieved maturity, but that he lives in a situation in which maturity is required of him but where he refuses to rise to the height of his calling. He is sinking back into becoming one of the masses whose characteristic is not "religionlessness" but superficiality.'[6]

Much of the secularism of the modern age is nothing more than another form of man's selfishness and man's pride.

This is not particularly new. Pride has traditionally been regarded as one of the seven deadly sins. And indeed it has been recognized as an evil for centuries before the sins of man were classified so neatly. Pride is as old as man himself. Man has always liked to think that he is autonomous. The first story in the Bible, after the creation story, is that of man's rebellion against God. And the

[6] Daniel Jenkins, *BR*, p. 36.

sorry account is continued in every age. It is not man's pride in his autonomy that is new but only its expression. The twentieth century has given it a form of its own. But the underlying attitude is neither modern nor praiseworthy. It is the old, old story of mankind and its sin.

It is not always noticed by those who espouse the new movement that their 'coming of age' does not necessarily mean the abolition of 'religion', even in the sense they give to the term 'religion'. It may mean no more than that the world produces a new religion. To quote Daniel Jenkins once more: 'The Enlightenment and the rise of science are no more than expressions of this maturity in certain realms of life. They may affect the way in which the man of faith exercises his responsibility in the world but in themselves they do not do away with the necessity for religion, if only because they themselves can become the agencies which can foster new religion, as was very clear in the case of the Enlightenment. The world's "coming of age" does not abolish religion. Both sin and faith will conspire to generate more religion out of this mature world and the man of faith will have to continue to vindicate his maturity in the only way which has always been possible, by renewed faith working through love.'[7]

What Jenkins makes clear here is that the spirit of the modern age is no more than a new expression of the same old spirit of man. And he goes on to point out that this new spirit can and does generate new 'religion'. Man loves his 'religion'. And even the modern secular man hugs to himself his religious illusions. It is a fallacy to think that his rejection of the Church means rejection of 'religion'.

[7] *BR*, p. 35.

CHAPTER FOUR

THE COMMON LIFE

THERE is a marked tendency among exponents of 'religionless Christianity' to stress the importance of what is commonly called the 'secular' over against the 'sacred' (though the very use of these terms cuts across what they are trying to say). In what looks like a reaction against the attitude which treated God as though He were the prisoner of the sanctuary there is a new emphasis on the truth that all of life belongs to God. He is to be discerned in the common life of men as well as in the religious life of men.

Sometimes this is expressed in 'one world' terminology, as when R. Gregor Smith says, 'So the division between the sacred and the profane was removed, the distinction between the religious and the secular, the difference between the shepherds and the sheep. Nothing was sacrosanct any more. The Old Testament and New Testament insight into the integrity of human life was recovered. Human life involved not two worlds, but one world; not a twofold system with nature and super-nature neatly dovetailed into one another, but one world, into which God's Word penetrated.'[1] No distinction is now made between the sacred and the secular. It is all one world, and the Christian is to live his life in that one world, not hovering doubtfully between two worlds, nor making frequent passages from one world to another. The unitary nature of Christian experience is emphasized, and there is a refusal to confine the 'spiritual' to any restricted part of life.

A widely quoted and very valuable statement of this point of view is Alec R. Vidler's discussion of what he

[1] *The New Man* (London, 1956), p. 45.

calls 'Holy Worldliness'.[2] He makes the point that the Christian lives a life of 'genuine worldliness'. This means 'living with men and serving them in all those areas where Christ is never named though they belong to him, or where he is named only to be misunderstood or reviled'.[3] The idea is that there is a wrong 'worldliness' but that this should not blind us to the fact that for the Christian there is also a right 'worldliness'. This world is God's world, and every part of life may accordingly be lived to His glory.

Now this is indeed true. Yet the rejection of the tendency to fragment can be taken too far. C. S. Lewis has an interesting statement in a passage in which he deals with A. R. Vidler's essay in *Soundings*. Lewis says, 'One must, however, walk warily, for the truth that *religion* as a department has really no right to exist can be misunderstood. Some will conclude that this illegitimate department ought to be abolished. Others will think, coming nearer to the truth, that it ought to cease to be departmental by being extended to the whole of life, but will misinterpret this. They will think it means that more and more of our secular transactions should be "opened with prayer", that a wearisomely explicit pietism should infest our talk, that there should be no more cakes and ale. A third sort, well aware that God still rules a very small part of their lives, and that "a departmental religion" is no good, may despair. It would have to be carefully explained to them that to be "still only a part" is not the same as being a permanent department. In all of us God "still" holds only a part. D-Day is only a week ago. The bite so far taken out of Normandy shows small on the map of Europe. The resistance is strong, the casualties heavy, and the event uncertain. There is, we have to admit, a line of demarcation between God's part in us and the enemy's region. But it is, we

[2] *Essays in Liberality* (London, 1957), pp. 95-112.
[3] *Op. cit.*, p. 111.

hope, a fighting line; not a frontier fixed by agreement.'[4]

It must be recognized that we are engaged in a conflict and that none of us is completely given over to God. It is simply not possible for us to live all of our life in all of its parts equally for God. Yet the ideal is there. We should not easily settle for a life any aspect of which is lived apart from God. All should be His. As Lewis also says, 'there is danger in the very concept of *religion*. It carries the suggestion that this is one more department of life, an extra department added to the economic, the social, the intellectual, the recreational, and all the rest. But that whose claims are infinite can have no standing as a department. Either it is an illusion or else our whole life falls under it.'[5]

That is why the new emphasis is to be welcomed. At the same time it ought not to be regarded as some profound new insight that we owe to 'religionless Christianity'. The theory of orthodox Christians has too often outrun their practice, but the teaching is plain enough. Thus the whole thrust of Oliver R. Barclay's *The Christian's Approach to University Life*[6] is directed towards showing that the Christian *ought* to take his full part in the secular activities of the University. Dr. Barclay says, 'It is not that a cultured Christian is a better Christian because of his culture, but he is, by and large, a more useful member of society and he is usually more robust and better able to withstand the strain of life. These things are given by God to mankind to make life richer and more pleasant, and to enable us to make fuller use of the natural resources of personality and material.'[7] The terminology is different. But there is the

[4] *Letters to Malcolm: Chiefly on Prayer* (London, 1964), pp. 47 f. [5] *Op. cit.*, p. 46. [6] London, 1963.
[7] *Op. cit.*, p. 25. *Cf.* also, 'We cannot safely launch out into a thoroughly secular society if we do not take care to maintain spiritual health. But too many Christians are afraid of being hurt. We must refuse the temptation to withdraw' (*op. cit.*, p. 24).

same full recognition that the Christian has no business to try to withdraw into a little world of the holy which he regards as all that matters. There is the same recognition that the whole of life is God's and that therefore the Christian must live it all to God's glory and not concentrate solely on a 'religious' sector.[8]

What is new in 'religionless Christianity', then, is not the idea that God is to be discerned in all of life. It is rather the thought that God is to be discerned in the common life of men as distinct from, perhaps even rather than in, the religious life of men. Men like Barclay find the 'sacred' as giving us the clue to the 'secular'. But some recent writers seem to reverse this.

This difference ought to be emphasized. The orthodox are quite clear that all of life is God's. There is no part of life of which the Christian can say 'This is the religious part of life; the rest does not concern God'. But he takes his relationship to God as primary, and therefore as the clue to the way he should conduct his secular affairs. This is not to say that he thinks the problems of living in the workaday world are all to be solved by 'religious' measures. A scientific problem must be tackled in a scientific way. A commercial problem is to be dealt with according to sound commercial practice. But whether he engages in science, technology, art, commerce or whatever he does, he engages in it as a Christian. Everything is part of the service of God. With George Herbert he sings:

[8] After I had written this I received a leaflet advertising a Convention sponsored by the Crusaders' Union. The general theme was advertised as 'One Life—Not Two', and the leaflet objected to making life 'a series of watertight compartments, in some of which God has no evident place'. It asked, 'Is this negative, inspired and restricted approach compatible with Christ's robust words, "I am come that you might have life, and have it more abundantly"?' It is plain that exponents of 'religionless Christianity' have no monopoly of the truth that life is one.

Teach me, my God and King,
    In all things Thee to see,
And what I do in anything
    To do it as for Thee!

A servant with this clause
    Makes drudgery divine;
Who sweeps a room, as for Thy laws,
    Makes that and the action fine.

Everything takes on new meaning because it is done for God. All of life is sacred.

What the new writers appear to be saying, by contrast, is that all of life is secular. It is life in the world that matters, and the sanctuary has relevance only when it bears on and fits men for life in the world. For them the 'secular' is the significant sphere. The specifically religious life is played down, and sometimes to all intents and purposes excluded from the significant encounter with God. Thus John Wren-Lewis can say, 'Prayer and mystical vision are real and important, but they cannot be the primary basis for religious conviction : this must come from *common* experience, and special experiences like prayer are only meaningful, in my view, insofar as they refer back to common experience.'[9] This appears to mean that the really significant part of life is the common life, the life which the Christian shares with the worldly man, the life which has no obvious relevance to the specifically 'religious'. The place of the specifically religious is not completely denied. Prayer and even 'mystical vision' are said to be 'real and important'. But Wren-Lewis says in so many words that these activities become meaningful only when they refer to common experience. It is the world's secular life which is the touchstone. Religious life is definitely subordinated to

⁹ *They Became Anglicans,* ed. Dewi Morgan (London, 1959), p. 175.

secular experience. It is the latter which gives the clue
to the former and not *vice versa*.

The idea that secular life is all important is taken to
its logical conclusion when it is brought into the interpretation of the service of Holy Communion. J. A. T.
Robinson complains that this service too often 'is not the
place at which the common and the communal point
through to the beyond in their midst, to the transcendent
in, with and under them, but precisely the opposite. It
ceases to be the holy meal, and becomes a religious service
in which we turn our backs on the common and the
community and in individualistic devotion go to "make
our communion" with "the God out there". This is the
essence of the religious perversion, when worship becomes
a realm into which to withdraw from the world to "be
with God"—even if it is only in order to receive strength
to go back into it'.[1] Bishop Robinson, however, maintains
that, 'The purpose of worship is not to retire from the
secular into the department of the religious, let alone to
escape from "this world" into "the other world", but to
open oneself to the meeting of the Christ in the common.'[2]

All this appears to mean that there is no particular
point in even such a solemn service as Holy Communion
except as it enables us to see the presence of Christ in the
common life. Indeed Bishop Robinson says as much: 'The
Holy Communion is the proclamation to the Church
and to the world that the presence of Christ with his
people is tied to a right receiving of the common, to a
right relationship with one's neighbour. For it is given
only in and through these things, both in church and out
of it.'[3] I do not see what these words mean unless that
we receive Christ in the common life or we do not receive
Him at all. The Holy Communion appears to be a way
of setting this truth forth symbolically. The idea that the
Holy Communion *in itself* is a means of drawing near to
God is firmly rejected.

[1] *HTG*, pp. 86 f.   [2] *HTG*, p. 87.   [3] *HTG*, p. 88.

This fails to reckon with the line of scriptural teaching that man *ought* to worship, a line of teaching that the Church has always regarded as important. It is set forth in its simplicity in the well-known words of the *Venite*. 'O come, let us worship and bow down: let us kneel before the Lord our maker,' sings the psalmist. Then, when he comes to give the reason for this, he says nothing about the common life or the like, but simply, 'For he is our God; and we are the people of his pasture, and the sheep of his hand' (Ps. 95: 6 f.). Ultimately there is no other reason for worship. Worship is acknowledging the worthship of God. It is not a means to an end, even if the end be as important as that of promoting the common life. Worship is an activity which centres on God, not on man.

Bonhoeffer's own position is never made clear. From prison he writes, 'it is remarkable how little I miss going to church. I wonder why'.[4] Evidently he felt little compulsion to worship. And evidently he got little out of worship, else he could not have said that he did not miss it much. In his 'Outline for a Book' he sketches in the main points, but when he comes to worship all he says is, '(d) Cultus. (Details to follow later, in particular on cultus and religion.)'.[5] It cannot be said that he loved to dwell on the place of worship as did his beloved psalmists.

There is a similar reluctance in many of those who advocate 'religionless Christianity'. Where they do give attention to worship they generally assess its value in terms of its usefulness in promoting the common life. They do not see worship as a duty to be practised for its own sake and not for any possible effects on man.

Yet this has been stressed again and again by the experts on worship. It is unfortunate that these modern writers simply ignore them. The point is made excellently, for example, in the opening chapters of Colin Dunlop's *Anglican Public Worship*.[6] He says, 'A justification of

[4] *Letters*, p. 54.   [5] *Letters*, p. 165.   [6] London, 1953.

worship on the grounds that it makes man more at home in this world, even if on the highest plane, is bound not only to fail, but to deceive. This is not to deny that the practice of worship enables a man the better to realize his role in this world as a stranger and a pilgrim who in a place of change and decay seeks a "city which hath foundations". But it only has these results when the eyes of the worshipper are fixed in faith upon that city and its Maker and not upon himself as existing independently of his eternal destiny.'[7] Again we read, 'There is a strong and wide tendency to try to justify public worship in ways which in the end do not justify it. This will always be the case when public worship is regarded as a means to some immediate end and not as an end in itself. This in fact is the first assertion that must be made in the justification of public worship. It is an activity which is its own justification. . . . To worship is to be true to oneself as one made in the image of God.'[8]

The modern liturgical movement has given rise to such widespread interest in worship that one wonders why these writers so consistently overlook this point. But overlook it they usually do. And their whole attitude to worship seems to be in flagrant contradiction to nineteen centuries of Christian experience. Century after century Christians have 'turned aside from the world' to find God. And they have found Him. According to these modern thinkers they ought not to have found Him. They had the wrong idea. They thought that they could enter the sanctuary of God and find God there. In their simplicity they thought that God might be expected to be found especially in His sanctuary. With Bishop E. H. Bickersteth they have sung:

'Come ye aside from all the world holds dear,
    For converse which the world has never known,

' *Op. cit.*, p. 10.   * *Op. cit.*, p. 13.

Alone with Me and with My Father here,
    With Me and with My Father not alone.

'Then, fresh from converse with your Lord, return
    And work till daylight softens into even :
The brief hours are not lost in which ye learn
    More of your Master and His rest in heaven.'

All this, we are now told, was wrong. It is true that there
are qualifications in some writers. Dr. Robinson, for
example, repeatedly says that the old formulations are
meaningful for some people, and once at any rate concedes that the older way of worship may help 'religious'
people.[9] But the logic of his position, and still more that
of Wren-Lewis and Bonhoeffer, is all against it. If 'the
presence of Christ with his people is tied to a right
receiving of the common' then it is tied to the right
receiving of the common. It is not found in a withdrawal
from the common. Dr. Robinson cannot have it both
ways.

And if God is to be found in the common life in such
a way that the divine presence is 'tied to a right receiving
of the common', if even the solemn service of Holy
Communion is only a way of pointing us to His presence
in common life, then the devout souls of earlier days
have gone the wrong way about it. They have looked for
God in the sanctuary, in times of withdrawal. They
should have looked in the common life to which the
presence is 'tied'.

It may be asked whether the Bishop of Woolwich does
not find more place for 'withdrawal' than I credit him
with. Perhaps he does. This is one of the points on which
he speaks with two voices. He agrees that there is a place
for church-going,[1] though not if the prevailing atmo-
sphere in a given church 'conveys the sense that people

[9] *HTG*, p. 91.
[1] *HTG*, p. 91.

actually go to church to *find* God'.[2] With this qualified approval of church-going we should set his refusal 'to doubt the virtue, and indeed the absolute necessity, for withdrawal'.[3] Against this he disapproves of the assumption that defines prayer 'in terms of what one does in the times of *dis*engagement',[4] and that 'the heart of prayer is withdrawal'.[5] He suspects that we 'have got to ask very seriously whether we should even begin our thinking about prayer in terms of the times we "set aside" . . . whether Christian prayer . . . is not to be *defined* in terms of penetration through the world to God rather than of withdrawal from the world to God'.[6] This looks like an explicit renunciation of withdrawal. And he certainly *does* say that the presence of Christ is 'tied' to the right receiving of the common.

Now, if the modern theologians are right, the way of withdrawal is not only not the best way to meet God. It is no way to meet God at all. It is a matter for blame, a crime for which they castigate the modern Church often, that it tries to meet God in this way, that it thinks it can find God in the sanctuary. There is no room for doubt on this point. It seems to be a principal aim of the writers of whom we are thinking to goad the Church into seeing that it will not find God in the holy place, but only in the common life. It must revise its thinking about the sanctuary, and revise it radically.

But generations of Christian people *have* found God in the quiet place. It would be the height of presumption and a monstrous distortion of the facts to maintain that Christian experience through all the centuries has been erroneous. And if generations of Christian men and

---

[2] *HTG*, p. 90; the words are quoted from J. Wren-Lewis and are introduced with 'we should have the courage to draw the consequences'.
[3] *HTG*, p. 93.
[4] *HTG*, p. 91.
[5] *HTG*, p. 92.
[6] *HTG*, p. 97 (Robinson's italics).

women have found God in this way the question arises, Why cannot we? Either the modern writers are correct, in which case the experience of the Church for centuries has been illusion. Or they are not correct, in which case we can still find God in the sanctuary. They do not seem to face this consequence of their position. They do not seem to see that they are engaging not so much in a further development of all previous Christian experience as in its negation. They give no real reason why we should think of them as being right and the whole previous Church of God as being wrong.

It is the same with private devotions as with public prayers. To quote Bishop Robinson again, the traditional view of private devotion rests on the view that 'the sacramental moments of communion with God are to be expected in the periods of withdrawal, which, like the camel's water, are to see one through the deserts of the day that must otherwise drain one dry. And even "arrow prayers" in the midst of the hurly burly presuppose an ejaculation, however momentary, *from* the pressures of the world *to* a God out there and above them all, with whom we can still hold communion *in spite of* them'.[7] All this is regarded as another version of the 'God of the gaps'. God, it is held, is thought by those who practise such devotions to be concerned in some aspects of life (the quiet time), but not in others (the hurly burly). Now, since the hurly burly makes up by far the greater part of living, this effectively excludes God from the larger part of life. In fact God is seen only in the 'religious' gaps. In most of life there is no place for Him.

Such contentions, whether about public worship or private prayer, ought to give us furiously to think. It can scarcely be denied that in recent years at any rate, the Church has often given the impression that the 'spiritual' can be distinguished from the 'secular', and that its busi-

[7] *HTG*, pp. 91 f. (Robinson's italics).

ness is with the 'spiritual'. It is of course held that it is a
duty of Christian men to live for Christ in the workaday
world. But attitudes have been taken up which seem to
imply that the ordinary world of everyday life is a barren
spiritual desert. A man must go there, but he must do so
in fear and trembling, having first laid in a bountiful
spiritual store from that which the Church provides. The
sphere where God can be met is one thing. The world is
quite another.

Christians have not meant to convey this impression,
but undoubtedly they have sometimes done so. With the
best will in the world they have acted in such a fashion
as to create the impression (sometimes subconsciously
even to hold it themselves) that a firm distinction can be
made between the sphere of ordinary life and the sphere
of the Church.

All this is very deplorable. All true Christians will
welcome the protest, and will take it as an occasion for
serious self-examination. We may well submit our actions
and motives to a close scrutiny to see how far we have
helped in propagating this error.

But this does not mean that we should go back on our
heritage. It is still true that millions of the very saints of
God have testified to the value of periods of withdrawal
and to the certainty that they have found God there. The
trouble with the modern movement is not that it insists
that God is in all of life. This has always been recognized
by Christians, even if their practice has not always
matched their theory. The trouble is that it seems to be
saying: 'God is in all of secular life. But He is not (or at
least not very much) in religious life.' It is rather like a
'God of the gaps' in reverse.

Thus the Bishop of Woolwich can say 'I am not greatly
excited by the current signs of the survival of religiousness
in Russia or of its revival in America'. He goes on to refer
to Oswald Spengler's view that the appearance of 'a
second religiousness' is the sign that a culture is drawing

near to the end of its life cycle. He doubts whether 'the main function of the Church is to make or to keep men religious'.[8] Earlier the Bishop has objected to the term 'organized religion' and he has said of this expression 'What a fearful phrase this is when one stops to think about it, and how calamitous that Christians should have come to find themselves committed to its defence'. He concedes that the Church has some concern with religion and that it must be organized. Then he goes on, 'But that Christianity should be equated in the public mind, inside as well as outside the Church, with "organized religion" merely shows how far we have departed from the New Testament. For the last thing the Church exists to be is an organization for the religious. Its charter is to be the servant of the world.'[9]

There can be nothing but cordial agreement with this last point. On any New Testament understanding of it the Church does not exist for its own benefit. It is concerned to minister in Christ's name to the world. It must never degenerate into an inward-looking holy club of like-minded souls.

But the Bishop seems to be saying more than that. When evidence of the survival of religion in Russia and its revival in America is not to be welcomed by the sincere Christian, then it is to be wondered what would be welcomed in those lands. The alternative to the survival of religion in Russia would appear to be its extinction. If by any chance Bishop Robinson is making a serious distinction between 'religiousness' and 'religion' at this

---

[8] *HTG*, pp. 138 f. *Cf.* also the article by Alec R. Vidler entitled, 'The Appalling Religiousness of America' (*op. cit.*, pp. 171–176). To anyone who knows conditions in both countries it will seem curious that Dr. Vidler can write, 'in Britain, while our churches are metaphorically if not literally falling into ruin, the disturbing and restoring presence of the living God is becoming an experienced reality amid the ruins. Here in the U.S.A., it seems to me, the cushion of religious efficiency and prosperity is still doing its comfortable, but fatal, work' (*op. cit.*, p. 173).

[9] *HTG*, pp. 133 f.

point, or perhaps between both of them and 'Christianity' it would be a help if he would say so.

Similarly with America. It is obvious to all, not least to the Americans themselves, that much is amiss in the religious life of that nation. The most searching criticisms of American religion have come from the Americans themselves. And when we consider the beam in our own eye we might be well advised to leave it at that. If we do want to go further we would do well rather to look for the significance of this movement into the churches of America than to waste our breath emphasizing its limitations. In any case, if it is true that much American religion is superficial, it is also true that in that country a very great number of people do meet together for the express purpose of worshipping God. And as they come together they place themselves under the sound of the gospel. If Christians are not to be 'excited' about this then he ought to say plainly what would excite him if it happened in America, and how this would take place apart from a revival of religion.

It seems to me that we do well to heed the remark of Daniel Jenkins, 'Church attendance is, of course, far from being the whole of Christian obedience but it is a form of distrust of the power of the Gospel to take it for granted that when people place themselves within sound of it they must necessarily resist or distrust it . . . in their proper anxiety not to fall victims of spiritual complacency, critically minded theologians almost reach the point of believing that the typical flourishing suburban church is, by definition, a conspiracy against God.'[1]

It is also worth our while to give some attention to the practical consequences of the depreciation of the specifically religious activities of the Church. If Christians are

[1] *BR*, p. 100. He also says, 'More evidence would be available on this point if the Gospel were more faithfully preached than it often is from the prosperous pulpits of the Western world' (*loc. cit.*).

to be discouraged in their 'religious' activities, and urged to concentrate on 'holy worldliness', then surely they will end up by being just as secular as is the world. Without trying to claim too much for worship and the like, it does at least have the effect of turning men's thoughts away from themselves and their activities to God. The same cannot be said about our secular pursuits. Advocates of 'religionless Christianity' do not seem to face the problem of how the secular world is to be won for Christ. If Christians are to attach maximum significance to their 'secular' activities and minimum significance to their 'religious' activities, will not the secular-minded be confirmed in their secularity? Will they not think that the root of the matter is in them already so that they have no need to conform their ways to the ways of Christ? Advocates of 'religionless Christianity' expressly affirm an evangelistic intent. They are trying to make the gospel relevant to modern man. It would be a help to those who are trying to understand them if they would tell us plainly what they understand by the gospel, and how it is to be commended to the world if Christians conform their ways to those of secular men.

Finally, let us notice the point made by Gregor Smith, when he speaks of 'the perennial temptation of every religion' to seek 'some secure foothold from which it may survey mankind, offering men consolation and assurance, indeed, but at the same time making it a condition of that offer that it itself, the religion, should be accepted along with these gifts, as the purveyor of them'.[2] Christianity, he thinks, has succumbed to this temptation. In the days of the early Church 'the fundamental concern was to express . . . unconditional concern for the historical needs of men. Since the coming of age of man in society, however, the fundamental concern has changed: the Church has sought to *preserve* its message, and with the message to preserve itself. It has sought to do this by

[2] *Op. cit.*, p. 54.

imposing itself and its message as an alien law on man's mind'.[3]

It may be doubted whether such a change as Gregor Smith posits has in fact taken place since man's 'coming of age'. What he is speaking of has surely always been the Church's temptation, and always to some extent she has succumbed to it. It is not a purely modern phenomenon. And, as with the division into sacred and secular, we can see how it has happened without condoning it. The Church has a message for mankind and it dare not say or do anything that would result in the loss of that message. But precisely because the message is so important it is all too easy to get things mixed and to concentrate on preserving the Church which passes on the message.

The importance of the message is the basic reason for the hesitation many feel about 'religionless Christianity'. It is not that they automatically reject new insights, but that they feel that this new movement is a way of rejecting the essential Christian gospel. It is fatally easy to confuse the Church which passes on the message with the message itself, and to feel that the Church as such is the thing to be preserved. It is not. It is the message that is all-important, and the Church is important only as the servant-Church, as the means of doing God's will in the world and bringing His gospel to the world that needs it. Believers must still hear the words of Christ: 'If any man will come after me, let him deny himself, and take up his cross daily, and follow me. For whosoever will save his life shall lose it: but whosoever will lose his life for my sake, the same shall save it' (Lk. 9: 23 f.). If we are candid we must confess with shame that we have all too often lost sight of this truth.

[3] *Op. cit.*, p. 55.

CHAPTER FIVE

THE IMPOSSIBILITY OF 'RELIGIONLESS CHRISTIANITY'

TOO often it does not appear to be realized that Christianity is impossible without 'religion' of some sort. It may be proper to distinguish between 'religion' and 'Christianity'. The essential part of the Christian faith is not something which can be reduced to any religious rites or ceremonies. It is something inward, an affair of the soul. Yet we have no grounds for believing that this inward state can exist without an outward expression in worship. It is not to be denied that an essential outward expression will be seen in common life. In the preceding section I have tried to make it clear that I am in full agreement with the contention that God is concerned with all of life, and that God's servant must likewise be concerned with all of life. It is quite impossible to divide life into two compartments labelling one 'sacred' and the other 'secular'. Unless we worship God in the common things of life by doing our daily work as part of our Christian service, and by regarding our social contacts also as part of our Christian service, we are not being true to the biblical understanding of Christianity. All this must be said, and the protest of modern theologians against the unnatural division of life into separate compartments must be welcomed.

Yet it is not true to say that there is no place for 'religion'. If it is true that the Christian man worships God in his daily work it is also true that he worships God in company with God's people in God's house. In doing this it is necessary for him to be clear what he is about. He must understand that religion all too easily degenerates into a sham, into a substitute for real Christianity. He must come to see that religion can keep men away from Christ. It can be a barrier to any real understanding of the Christian way. But this does not mean that he must abandon 'religion'. Rather it means that he must find the right place for 'religion' and the right form of 'religion'.

For the fact is that, more often than not, true faith arises from religion. Occasionally faith may be generated in individuals by other means, but for almost all of us it arises in one way or another from religious activity. Many of us have been brought up from infancy to go to church and Sunday school. We were taught at our mother's knee to say our prayers, and from an early age we were accustomed to read the Bible. We have gone to church and heard the faith expounded. These things have not meant very much to us perhaps. They have been completely outward. They are things we have done because we were told to do them, and not because we either wanted to or because we understood what they meant.

But they did accustom us to the great ideas of Christianity. They did set before us something other than the world's way of living. Then one day there dawned in on us an understanding of what these things meant. With some of us this took place in a moment of time. With others of us it occurred gradually, perhaps over a period of years. What had happened was that we entered into a realization of the 'faith' to which the 'religion' we had been accustomed to pointed. Faith was born out of religion.

This is the case also with those who have not had a godly upbringing. Some of us have come into contact with the gospel for the very first time in adult life. We have heard it preached by an evangelist, or we have seen it lived by some humble Christian. We have been led to enquire further and in this way have come to know what faith is. But again, what started us out along the

road of faith was a prior 'religious' activity, in this case
in someone other than ourselves.

It may well be that, on occasion, faith arises without
any prior 'religious' activity (though it is hard to envisage
this happening with any frequency, if at all). If those who
uphold 'religionless Christianity' are prepared to cite
examples, then I am prepared to listen. But what is
abundantly clear to me is that the people I know who
possess a right Christian faith were brought to it by
activity of the kind which I can only call 'religious'.

Now let us notice that those who are foremost in
promoting 'religionless Christianity' are usually insistent
on the central place that is to be given to love. Rites and
ceremonies are of little importance. Christian love is
central. To secure this point they will often relegate
dogma to a secondary place, if that. It would, I think,
not be an overstatement to affirm that the new movement
is an undogmatic one. But in the New Testament ethical
conduct, and specifically Christian love, are not regarded
as rootless. They are demanded (and possible) only
because the great Christian dogmas are true. The same
man wrote the Epistle to the Romans and 1 Corinthians
13. And we are wrong if we think of him as dealing with
different realities in these two places. The hymn in praise
of love is for Paul the natural outworking of the position
he takes up in Romans.

It appears that now we are being asked to do the
equivalent of accepting 1 Corinthians 13 while maintain-
ing that Romans is optional. But if we neglect the dog-
matic structure of Romans why should we retain the
love which is its offspring? And how?

Another question arises from all this. Why should we
encourage any specifically Christian attitudes? The
'religionless' man appears to be the ideal towards which
this movement is striving. The work of Christians is to
be discerned, not in the sanctuary, but in the forum, in
the market-place. Christians are to realize the central

importance of 'the common life' and to get alongside men there. But if those who name the name of Christ become 'religionless' we may ask what is the point of it all? Is not the world able to reach the blessed state quite apart from 'religion'? Are we not to say that the salt has lost its savour? By becoming 'religionless' Christians have surely forfeited that which is distinctive and have become exactly like other men.

It might perhaps be retorted that Christians should be distinctive, not by being 'religious' but by being 'Christian', *i.e.* by producing qualities of character like love. This, however, would not solve my problem. I should then want to know whether the love in question is love with a specifically Christian content, or whether it is to be understood as a completely secular phenomenon. If the latter, there is clearly no place for Christianity. If the former, I wonder how the specifically Christian content is to be preserved apart from its context in the whole Christian scheme of things, and that includes Christian doctrine and Christian worship.

But 'religionless Christianity' appears to mean the abandonment of any real emphasis on Christian doctrine and worship. The question then arises, What contribution have Christians to make to the new world that is to arise? It seems to me that the logic of 'religionless Christianity' is that the Christian Church has no great role to play. Maybe it hasn't. But if this is what its advocates mean, why do they not say so? And if they do not mean this, would they please make plain exactly what they do mean? If we are to have no religion it is difficult to see what importance we are to attach to the Church. But if we feel that despite its weakness and often faithlessness the Church still has a word to say to a secular, materialistic world, then it would seem that we must not take 'religionless Christianity' too far.

We must also face the fact that faith invariably issues in religion. Jenkins has this to say: 'As he himself' (*i.e.*

Barth) 'insists, genuine faith issues in religion. There is a true Christian religion. The more fully alive faith is, the more it is honoured and blessed by God, the more richly and vigorously it produces a heritage of religion with which those who inherit it have to come to terms. This fact shows how misleading it is to regard religion as the affair of the godless man alone. If that were so, the situation would be simpler. The dilemma becomes most acute when it is seen that religion is also so much the affair of the godly man.'[1]

This must be faced. It is an oversimplification to say that we must look for a Christianity without 'religion'. If we could simply reject religion, lock, stock and barrel, we would know where we were. But it is part of our dilemma that true faith always issues in religion. We cannot accordingly reject religion. We are called upon to do something much harder. We must distinguish between true and false religion.

The impossibility of Bonhoeffer's programme is recognized by such a friendly critic as Walter Harrelson. He asks, 'Must it not also be said that a nonreligious interpretation of biblical faith would soon become another religion, another form within which biblical faith was enshrined?' He goes on, 'This is for me the pathos in the call of Bonhoeffer for a secular reinterpretation of biblical terminology. Biblical faith would have undergone only one more effort of men to interpret its meaning in another set of terms. The nonreligious age which the Western world has entered does of course have its important differences from other ages, but it is not so different from other ages as to require, or to allow for, the break with religion which Bonhoeffer proposes. Should the program be realized, we should soon see

---

[1] *BR*, pp. 32 f. Later he has this warning, 'The Church may indeed spend too much of her time today in making "insiders" comfortable, but the way to protest against this is not by dramatizing oneself as a more Christian "outsider"' (*op. cit.*, p. 117).

another religion—a *nonreligious* religion—with its new terminology, its new cultic acts, its fresh set of ethical and cultural understandings and mandates.'[2]

This should be more widely recognized than it is. Those who call for 'religionless Christianity' are making an impossible demand. If they were successful they would simply replace one form of religion by another. And since they apparently do not realize that they would be creating a new 'religion', we have scant hope that the new would be an improvement on the old.

Appeal is often made to St. Paul when the place of religion is discussed. It is suggested that he was brought up as a very religious man, a model of what an adherent of the Jewish religion should be. Yet he had to learn that he must give up his trust in circumcision and the like and cast himself unreservedly on God's mercy in Christ. This meant an abandonment of his earlier 'religion' with all its law-keeping and ceremonies. The suggestion is that modern man must likewise cast aside his 'religion'. Like Paul he must learn to live by faith.

There is truth and error here. It is true that Paul learned not to trust in his 'religion'. He did learn to live by faith. In both these respects we must follow him. It is not easy to abandon the religious props on which we have always leant and to cast ourselves unreservedly on the grace of God. But this is a necessity if we are to be Christians in the New Testament sense.

But when all this has been said it still remains that Paul did not live as a 'religionless' man. As a Christian, if the New Testament picture of him is at all reliable, he was profoundly religious. We see him constantly engaging in specific religious activities and inculcating these on others. He was frequently found worshipping in the synagogues as well as in assemblies of Christians. He prayed. He read

[2] *The Place of Bonhoeffer*, ed. Martin E. Marty (London, 1963), p. 138. He adds, 'But the effort is still profoundly worthwhile.'

the Bible. He was very active in what we would call 'church' work. This must always be borne in mind when appeal is made to St. Paul. It is not true that he abandoned religion. It is true that he put it in its right place.

Perhaps this is the place to notice that Bonhoeffer's views must have been influenced, perhaps strongly, by his environment. Thus he lived in very difficult days, with the great depression, the rise of the Nazi movement in Germany, and the war. Such things cause James Richmond to say, 'Living so close to the frightful excesses of "adult" twentieth-century man, he would naturally come to regard any alleged innate religious awareness as nonsense . . . it may be that untypical times give rise to unbalanced theories of human nature.'[3]

Richmond sees a further factor in the growth of the Barthian movement with its anti-religious and anti-philosophical emphasis. This saw Christianity as concerned only with 'that act by which God in his grace disclosed himself to religionless and godless man as though he were a cat or a stick or a stone'. He proceeds, 'This "religionless" view of man virtually came to be regarded as orthodoxy in the 'thirties during the German Confessional Church's struggle with Nazi immanentism (the idea of a divine self-disclosure in race), in which that Church felt compelled to deny all alleged "secondary revelations" in human nature, race and history, which it opposed by a "christocentric" view of revelation. This led to an official ecclesiastical victory for the religionless doctrine of man of the extreme Dialectical theologians, expressed in the celebrated Declaration of Barmen of May, 1934.'[4]

This background was not without influence on Bonhoeffer. The 'religionless' view of man does not appear to be a strikingly original contribution of his own (though the particular form in which he expressed it was his own). It was one of the accepted ideas in Germany at the time

[3] *Four Anchors*, p. 37. [4] *Op. cit.*, p. 38.

and an idea which he was strongly predisposed to take over. This does not, of course, mean that it is wrong. But it does mean that we ought to be clear as to why Bonhoeffer came to hold it if we are to evaluate its significance correctly.

Further, the 'religion' in his 'religionless' Christianity is not necessarily that which we would naturally understand by the term. To cite Richmond once more, 'by "religion" he seems to have understood not merely that exaggerated immanentism characteristic of nineteenth-century German theology. He meant also something terribly Teutonic, a frightfully individualistic pietism, an other-worldly sectarianism which regarded itself as at war with the world and which linked itself to a Prussian moralism which frowned suspiciously upon innocent worldly intercourse and enjoyment'.[5] This does not mean that Bonhoeffer rejected this particular form of religion and left room for another. He did not. He is quite explicit that he sees no place in the future for *any* religion. All that Richmond is saying is that, though Bonhoeffer reacted against all religion, the only form in which he actually knew and understood religion was this 'other-worldly sectarianism'.

When we talk about 'religion' we do not usually have in mind anything like this. For us 'religion' is a broader and a deeper thing. Accordingly it is doubtful how far Bonhoeffer's strictures apply to our very different contemporary scene. In fact when we consider the abnormal times during which Bonhoeffer's thought was formed, the way in which the 'religionless' concept was so widely dominant in the theological thought of his day, and the different understanding of 'religion' that he had, it is hard to resist the impression that his ideas cannot apply to the contemporary scene without a lot of translation. And this the advocates of 'religionless Christianity' do not seem to have provided.

[5] *Op. cit.*, p. 39.

care is takin to see that we do not transgress the dicta of the scientists or the philosophers (the theologians do not appear to matter). When the world as a whole finds it difficult to accept traditional Christianity the principle of Christianity would into what traditional Christianity teachos, but to modern

CHAPTER SIX

A MAN-CENTRED WORLD?

IT seems to many critics of the movement we are discussing that all too prominent a place is given to man. Indeed the question arises in their minds, Is not the system we are being asked to accept one which is completely anthropo-centric? Sometimes this appears to be admitted in so many words, as when H. A. Williams speaks of discovering 'how a man's knowledge of God and his attitude towards God are affected by his growing awareness of what he is and how he functions as a psychic entity. This of course will have important results in his subsequent statement of how any Christian doctrine is to be understood'.[1] This is typical. The point of reference is in man, especially in modern man.

Bonhoeffer can define being a Christian in completely non-religious, even, if the paradox be permitted, in non-Christian terms. 'To be a Christian does not mean to be religious in a particular way, to cultivate some particular form of asceticism (as a sinner, a penitent or a saint), but to be a man.'[2] I do not find it difficult that he eschews this or that specifically Christian act, or that he inculcates an attitude of acceptance of one's destiny as a man. But I do find it difficult that he eschews all Christian acts, and says nothing at all of faith in Christ (he does speak of 'faith' later on, but it is a 'participation in the suffering of God in Christ';[3] there is no mention of faith in Christ). It is all so depressingly man-centred. 'To be a man' is the whole definition of 'Christian'.

The utterances, the thoughts, the progress of man are treated by these writers with the utmost respect. Every

[1] *Soundings*, pp. 72 f.
[2] *Letters*, p. 123.　　　　　　　　[3] *Loc. cit.*

care is taken to see that we do not transgress the dicta
of the scientists or the philosophers (the theologians do
not appear to matter quite so much!). When the world as
a whole finds it difficult to accept traditional Christianity
the remedy appears to be not to educate the world into
what traditional Christianity means, but to modify traditional Christianity so that it becomes acceptable to the
world. Thus E. L. Mascall can complain that the contri-
butors to *Soundings* 'seem for the most part to be more
confident in the contemporary world's estimate of the
realities of the human situation than they are in the great
tradition of thought and life that they have inherited as
members of the Church'.[4] More thought might certainly
have been given to the understanding of Christianity
that has emerged in the Church through nineteen
centuries of thinking about the faith and trying to live it
in however blundering a fashion. Granted that the
Church has made mistakes, it is still astonishing that a
group of Christian writers should be so ready to take the
world on trust and to reject the Church practically in its
entirety.

No serious attempt is made to justify this taking of
modern man as the supreme criterion. Yet on the face of
it it is far from obvious that modern man is worthy of
this place. In this connection Jenkins can refer to the
position of Paul Tillich in this way : 'It is not surprising
that Tillich never says precisely who this modern man
is, or what makes his questions so particularly authorita-
tive, or why they should be different in kind from the
questions posed by ancient man, or what their relation
is to the questions posed by God to man in his self-
revelation.'[5]

---

[4] *Up and Down in Adria* (London, 1963), p. 12.
[5] *BR*, *p.* 57. He goes on to point out that Tillich's ' "God
above God" can quickly cease to be the hidden God revealed in
Christ who retains his freedom in the revelation; it can become
no more than the name given by the theologian to the vitality
produced by his own interest in his subject, an interest which

It is moreover the case that 'religionless Christianity' places no stress on God's saving activity in Christ. This has always been regarded as central to Christianity but not only is it not mentioned, there seems no place for it in the new scheme of things. If Christianity is to be 'religionless' then what place is there for an atoning act? As Bonhoeffer states the case men are not asked to repent and seek their salvation in what God has done for them in Christ. They are simply to rise to their full secular stature. Not for nothing has the new movement been called Pelagian (though that heretic did find more scope for God than do these moderns!).

The fact ought to be faced that, as we saw earlier,[6] though modern man has made tremendous advances in the fields of science and technology he has not been conspicuously successful in other realms of life. This is not really an outstanding age in the production of great art, or great literature, nor can it fairly be said that this is an age when man has attained great heights morally. But why the men of science or the technologists should be given the decisive voice in matters religious is not apparent.

Some modern writing gives the impression that, compared to the scientists, men of religion are limited in outlook. Thus J. S. Habgood can say, 'In an age when the perspectives of space and time have been bewilderingly enlarged, when man has been shown new depths in himself by psychology, and has radically revised his

remains merely aesthetic even when it contemplates the very abyss of meaninglessness. Tillich's theology operates on too profound a level for him to fall into this danger himself, but its failure to lead men directly to confrontation with the revelation of the living God as declared by the men of the Bible never finally lays the suspicion that this might, after all, be interpreted as no more than a very sophisticated form of religious humanism' (*BR*, pp. 57 f.). Alisdair Macintyre is not so kind. He maintains that, 'Even if we were to concede Tillich a verbal triumph over the atheist, the substance of atheism has been conceded' (*HTGD*, p. 220). [6] See above pp. 39 f.

estimate of his place in nature by seeing himself in his
evolutionary context, there is a danger of ordinary
religious symbolism appearing trivial.'[7] Men have the
idea that in the modern world religion is stodgy and it
is the new ideas which are brilliant, striking, attractive.
Our new theological writers sometimes convey the
impression (whether they mean to or not) that traditionally-minded Christians are dull, whereas the adven-
turous ideas they themselves put out are in a different
category.[8] They might heed some words of E. L. Mascall,
'Dr. Habgood points to the impression, widely given, that,
compared with that of science, the vision of theology
often seems narrow and less evocative in its images. True
once more, but, as I have said in discussing Mr. Root's
essay, the fault is in Christians and not in the Faith and,
with all respect, I must say that the Leadsmen seem to
me to be every bit as drab in their outlook as their
fellow-Christians and fellow-theologians.'[9] These are
perhaps hard words, but they needed to be said.

Not only is there a supreme place given to modern man
which requires justification, but also there is a striking
omission of some notes which have always been regarded
as integral to real religion. One of these is the note of
penitence. This is scarcely mentioned in most treatments.
Thus the index to *Honest to God* makes no reference to
repentance or penitence, though this may not be signifi-

---

[7] *Soundings*, p. 28.

[8] Thus Barbara Thiering, writing in the Australian church
paper, *The Anglican*, under the heading 'We Cannot Ignore
This Revolution' (Nov. 7, 1963) says, 'To accept this fact (*i.e.*
that our culture will pass) is an inevitable part of the human
adventure, and to commit ourselves to a past age, denying our
own, is to run the risk of putting an end to that adventure altogether.' She uses adjectives like 'courageous' and nouns like
'faith' and 'liberty' to describe the new thinkers, whereas the
orthodox resent 'any disturbance of the venerable theological
mould in which their minds were set'. But all this is to beg the
question.

[9] *Op. cit.*, pp. 26 f. 'Leadsmen' is Mascall's word for the con-
tributors to *Soundings*.

cant as the index is so condensed; the book, however, has little to say on these topics. There is but one reference under the two headings in *Soundings* and in it H. A. Williams is regretting 'the fundamental mistake often made in exhortations to repentance and amendment. They attempt to confirm me in my lack of faith by getting me to organize the self I know against the self I do not know. The result is that growth in self-awareness is inhibited.'[1] It cannot be held that this indicates a profound interest in and concern for penitence. Elsewhere Williams explains repentance in these terms: 'Stop doing a, b, c. Tell God you are sorry for doing them and start trying to do x, y, and z. The possibility of vision is excluded from the start. The path of increasing awareness is blocked.'[2] In passing, one would have thought that even a Cambridge don would be aware that this is a caricature! But the important thing is that Williams finds no place for genuine repentance. Rather he puts all his emphasis on 'awareness'. Should not this be labelled Gnosticism? At any rate it has scant claim to be considered Christian.

The impression left by reading a good deal of modern literature is that the Church has good reason to be penitent. It has gone in for 'religion'. It has read its Bible and said its prayers and preached its sermons. But it has failed to discharge its task in the world, we are told, and therefore it should fall down on its knees before God.

In the measure in which the indictment is true the Church ought to be penitent. But is there not a necessity also for calling on the world to repent of its pride, its arrogance, its inhumanity, and all the rest? Why should

---

[1] *Op. cit.*, p. 90. He has earlier complained bitterly about the confessions of sin in the Book of Common Prayer (*op. cit.*, p. 79). Such views seem to presuppose inadequate ideas about the nature of sin, and these, too, find expression, *e.g.* 'The root of sin, as we have seen, is the identification of my total self with the self of which I am aware' (*op. cit.*, p. 95).

[2] *Objections to Christian Belief* (Cambridge, 1963), p. 48.

the irreligious be exempt from the call to repentance?
Our Lord, like John the Baptist before Him, and His
apostles after Him, began His ministry by saying to men
'repent' (Mk. 1: 15; Mt. 3: 2; 4: 17; Mk. 6: 12; Acts
2: 38). One would feel a good deal happier about the
modern movement if there were clear evidence that it
were rebuking the world as well as the Church. The
suspicion is left that there is not much wrong with the
world. It is difficult to see how this can be squared with
biblical teaching.[3]

For the Bible consistently regards men as having gone
astray from the right path. From Genesis 3 onwards man
is regarded as a sinner, and he is consistently called on to
repent. The New Testament uses such expressions as conversion and the new birth. Paul employs the imagery of
dying and rising again, and of putting off the old man
and putting on the new. These are not shorthand ways
of saying that all will be well with the natural man if he
will only rise to his full stature. They are ways of saying
that the natural man is on the wrong track altogether.
They represent a call for radical, total renewal. This note
of challenge is desperately important in the New Testament. But it is practically absent from the writings of
the new movement.

A good deal is made of the importance of honest doubt.
We often find the words of Tennyson quoted 'there lives
more faith in honest doubt . . . than in half the creeds'.

[3] A very rare example of a willingness to see the world as
coming short is the passage in which R. Gregor Smith, after
calling on the Church to confess 'that it has too long regarded
the sphere of history as one which it is called to govern and
control' looks for 'the readiness of the adult mature world, on
the other hand, to perceive the ground of its work and hope in
the same history, a history which carries with it unconditional
validity' (*The New Man*, London, 1956, p. 64). This is to be
welcomed as an unusual recognition that all is not well with the
natural man. It is not, of course, an adequate statement of the
demand that Scripture makes for a radical re-birth of the natural
man.

This is made the excuse for doubting most things that Christianity has traditionally taught. It is worth noting in passing that Tennyson did not say 'in all the creeds' but 'in half the creeds'. Apparently he was prepared to concede that in fact the creeds contain a great deal of truth.

Now 'honest' doubt is not a commodity in plentiful supply. Doubt there is in plenty but it is all too easy to doubt for the wrong reasons. Sometimes we meet with the 'doubt' of the scientific man who is simply not prepared to concede the possibility of the religious hypothesis. He accepts 'scientific truth' but in practice gives little place to any other. There is the 'doubt' of Daniel Jenkins' 'self-consciously "liberal" preacher', a man 'who is constantly drawing unfavourable contrasts between the men of the Old Testament and "the ages of faith" on the one hand and his own enlightened congregation on the other, and who dramatizes himself as a man of exceptional courage because he refuses to make up his mind over matters which most Christians believe call inescapably for decision, celebrating eloquently Sunday by Sunday his ability to seek for but never to arrive at the truth'.[4] It is of course the case that many 'liberal' preachers do not come under Jenkins' strictures. But it can scarcely be denied that there are some who do. It is simply not the case that dishonest doubt is confined to orthodox Christians. Many others, both inside and outside the Church, share this fault, though the manner in which their 'doubt' is expressed varies.

And in any case 'honest doubt' is throughout regarded with respect as a praiseworthy activity of autonomous man. No serious consideration is given to the possibility that God may have revealed Himself so plainly that the really honest man will usually recognize this and accept the revelation. By contrast, C. S. Lewis has an interesting passage in which he makes one of his characters say: 'Let

[4] *BR*, pp. 63 f.

us be frank. Our opinions were not honestly come by. We simply found ourselves in contact with a certain current of ideas and plunged into it because it seemed modern and successful. At College, you know, we just started automatically writing the kind of essays that got good marks and saying the kind of things that won applause. When, in our whole lives, did we honestly face, in solitude, the one question on which all turned: whether after all the Supernatural might not in fact occur? When did we put up one moment's real resistance to the loss of our faith?'[5] Lewis does not suggest of course that all unorthodox thinkers are like this. Nor do I. But the fact must be faced that not all who forsake orthodoxy do so for adequate reasons. The converse to this is that those who hold firmly to orthodoxy are not necessarily intellectually dishonest. The resolution of 'honest doubt' may well issue in a firmer commitment to orthodoxy. It is presumption for anyone to hold that all really honest doubters will end up agreeing in substance with his point of view.

Christians for centuries have believed that God has not left Himself without adequate witness. What I find depressing is the fact that so many who profess and call themselves Christians pay so little attention to the claims of revelation and so much to the dicta of modern men.

All the more is this relevant in view of the very tentative nature of many of the conclusions of modern scientists and others.[6] The typical modern scientist is a much more humble person than one would gather from reading the literature of 'religionless Christianity'. He is much less sure that his conclusions will stand for ever, and much more ready to agree that the 'religious' view of the world may have something to be said for it.

---

[5] *The Great Divorce* (London, 1945), pp. 37 f.
[6] See D. Martyn Lloyd-Jones, *The Approach to Truth: Scientific and Religious* (London, 1963).

CHAPTER SEVEN

EVANGELISM

UPHOLDERS of the idea of religionless Christianity often stress the evangelistic importance of what they are doing. Indeed sometimes it appears that their primary interest is in evangelism. Their distress at the picture presented by traditional Christianity arises in large measure because they feel it is a hindrance to the spread of the gospel. So long as men keep mouthing the old platitudes and presenting ideas which have long ago been discarded by the world at large as authentic Christianity, so long the message of the gospel will never be heeded other than by a tiny minority.

Bonhoeffer sees traditional evangelism and its failure in this way: 'God thus became the answer to life's problems, the solution of its distresses and conflicts. As a result, if anyone had no such difficulties, if he refused to identify himself in sympathy with those who had, it was no good trying to win him for God. The only way of getting at him was to show that he had all these problems, needs and conflicts without being aware of it or owning up to it. Existentialist philosophy and pyschotherapy have both been pretty clever at this sort of thing. It is then possible to talk to a man about God, and methodism can celebrate its triumph. If, however, it does not come off, if a man won't see that his happiness is really damnation, his health sickness, his vigour and vitality despair; if he won't call them what they really are, the theologian is at his wits' end. He must be a hardened sinner of a particularly vicious type. If not, he is a case of bourgeois complacency, and the one is as far from salvation as the other.'[1]

[1] *Letters*, pp. 114 f.

The trouble appears to be that traditional evangelism has tried to make men in one mould. It has seen all their variety as a drab uniformity, and has nothing to offer the man who does not see himself as a sinner. So Bonhoeffer is looking for a way of presenting Christianity which takes men as they are. If they are happy and healthy and vigorous and vital, then none of this should be interfered with in the interests of a traditional apologetic.

We must agree with some of this. Traditional apologetic has no rights. Men must not be made to conform to it. Yet the question remains, Is Bonhoeffer trying to present the essential message of Jesus? Or is he telling worldly, secular man that because he does not feel that anything is amiss nothing is amiss? The New Testament regards man, no matter how great his pride and self-satisfaction, as a sinner. Are we now to say that this is non-essential? That Christ really has no message for the man who feels happy and healthy and vigorous and vital? If he does not feel that he is a sinner are we to assure him that everything is all right, that he is to keep on being happy and the rest of it and not worry about sin? It is a new thing this, that the message of the gospel is for those who feel their sinfulness only, and that those who think they are healthy must necessarily be healthy. It was not in this way that the Christian Church first tackled the job of proclaiming the gospel.

It is true that Bonhoeffer occasionally recognizes that men are sinners, but he never tells us what should be done about it. This is the kind of thing he says, 'it must be said that man is certainly a sinner, but not mean or common, not by a long chalk. To put the matter in the most banal way, are Goethe or Napoleon sinners because they were not always faithful husbands? It is not the sins of weakness, but the sins of strength, which matter here. It is not in the least necessary to spy out things. The

Bible never does so.'[2] But what follows? Bonhoeffer
never says what Goethe and Napoleon should do about
their 'sins of strength'. Are such sins serious? And why
should Goethe and Napoleon be allowed to be unfaithful
husbands?

This is really all most unsatisfactory. Men may make
distinctions between classes of sinners, regarding 'mean
or common' sins as serious and looking differently
at 'sins of strength'; but the Bible does not. The Bible
sees all sin as serious. And so does common sense. We
cannot allow Goethe and Napoleon to be unfaithful
husbands and forbid lesser men to indulge themselves.
A weakening of the doctrine of sin may suit modern
men. But it cannot be made the basis of a satisfactory
theology.

Others share Bonhoeffer's view that traditional ways
of presenting the gospel will no longer suffice. Thus the
Bishop of Woolwich affirms his conviction that 'we are
being called, over the years ahead, to far more than a
restating of traditional orthodoxy in modern terms'. He
proceeds, 'Indeed, if our defence of the Faith is limited
to this, we shall find in all likelihood that we have lost
out to all but a tiny religious remnant.'[3] This conviction
lies behind much of what he has written as appears
again and again through his book. Sometimes he utters
orthodox sentiments. But characteristically he says that
orthodoxy will not do (this contradiction is one of the
reasons why his book is so hard to understand, and why
he complains that people misrepresent him). It must be
abandoned, and that not only in its expression, but also
in its content, if the gospel is to be commended to this
generation and, especially, to those that lie ahead.

Similarly H. E. Root can say, 'The greatest intellectual
challenge to faith is simply that thoroughly secularized
intelligence which is now the rule rather than the

[2] *Letters*, p. 118.
[3] *HTG*, p. 7.

exception, whether it expresses itself in science or philosophy or politics or the arts. It is by no means clear that
anything like Christian faith in the form we know it will
ever again be able to come alive for people of our own
time or of such future time as we can imagine.'[4] This is
plain enough. Orthodoxy is doomed. A radical reshaping
is the price of survival. There is an unshakable pessimism
about the prospects of orthodox Christianity.

One thing that is not always noticed is that in this
respect our 'advanced' thinkers show themselves thoroughly conservative. An almost precisely similar pessimism has been in evidence, and has been advanced with
equal confidence, at practically every period of the
Church's history. Thus in 1736 Bishop Butler recorded
the judgment of many in his day: 'It is come, I know not
how, to be taken for granted, by many persons, that
Christianity is not so much as a subject of inquiry; but
that it is, now at length, discovered to be fictitious. And
accordingly they treat it, as if, in the present age, this
were an agreed point among all people of discernment;
and nothing remained, but to set it up as a principal
subject of mirth and ridicule.'[5] Such quotations could
be multiplied. It is traditional with a certain type of
'advanced' thinker that Christianity is not intellectually
respectable. It may be ridiculed or discarded. Its demise
is at hand. The one thing that must not be done with it is
to take its orthodox expression seriously.

But why should the critics of orthodoxy be regarded as
almost certainly right? They are most of them eminent
enough academically and they command respect as
thinkers. But is this enough? The essence of Christianity
is something which may be hidden from the wise, but
revealed to the simple. There is a significant passage in
Lecky in which he comments on the way the thinkers
of the ancient world regarded Christianity. 'That the

[4] *Soundings*, p. 6.
[5] *Advertisement*, prefixed to *The Analogy of Religion*.

greatest religious change in the history of mankind', he says, 'should have taken place under the eyes of a brilliant galaxy of philosophers and historians, who were profoundly conscious of the decomposition around them, that all of these writers should have utterly failed to predict the issue of the movement they were observing, and that, during the space of three centuries, they should have treated as simply contemptible an agency which all men must now admit to have been, for good or for evil, the most powerful moral lever that has ever been applied to the affairs of man, are facts well worthy of meditation in every period of religious transition.'[6] It is not the case, of course, that the theologians we have in mind are on all fours with Lecky's philosophers and historians. The only point of the comparison is that it is possible for brilliant minds to go wildly astray in their estimate of Christianity. Certainly we should consider carefully what our leaders of thought have to say. But we must also recognize that outstanding academics and brilliant thinkers are not necessarily the best judges of a spiritual movement.

This does not mean, of course, that we should adopt an obscurantist position. In every generation the challenge of 'advanced' thinkers is to be taken seriously, and we should all take the present challenge with the seriousness it deserves. But it is important to see the contentions of the new thinkers for what they really are, and not for what they are not. They are not something strikingly new and original, which will hit the Church hard because she has hitherto had no experience of this kind of thing. In every generation she has faced something of the sort. If the present challenge to orthodoxy is to be accepted as decisive, as giving orthodoxy that death-blow that no previous challenge has succeeded in administering, then someone ought to show that it differs

[6] W. E. H. Lecky, *History of European Morals*, I (London, 1911), p. 338.

in kind from all previous challenges. For, though it is being urged as strikingly new (and it is indeed garnished with novel trimmings), underneath it is very much the mixture as before. The fundamental thing, the basic attitude, is that which we have seen through the centuries. It is an uncritical readiness to accept what 'modern' man says as determinative. 'Modern' man cannot accept orthodoxy. Therefore orthodoxy must go. This has been repeated *ad lib.* and *ad nauseam.*

The present restatement of the basic position of the sceptics relies heavily on the notion of secularism. 'Modern' man is thoroughly secularized. Therefore he will never accept orthodox Christianity. Therefore orthodox Christianity must be replaced by something up to date. But why the Church should accept the views of secular man as decisive is never shown. Yet if the new position is to be accepted it must be.

Nicholas Mosley well brings out the error in much modern writing when he says, 'The basic false assumption is that the Church has to make contact with the world by assuming the world's characteristics. There is no logic in this, certainly no evidence. The whole Bible is against it. The story of the New Testament is passionately, agonisingly against it.'[7] It is a fruitful exercise to meditate on the significance of the cross. Christians have always seen in the cross the decisive action of God for man's salvation. But who among those who reverently contemplate the agony of Gethsemane and Calvary can easily accept the view that secular man is saved in his secularity, that there is no need for religion or for confronting secular man with the challenge to repent, to deny himself, and to take up his cross and follow Christ?

It is true that the Church is under an obligation to talk with the world in a way that the world can understand. It is true that the Church ought to be respectful

[7] *Prism,* Oct. 1962, p. 2.

of the achievement of the secular world, and ought not to try to pervert this with a view to bringing the secular world somehow under the control and direction of the Church's preconceived notions. But it is also true that there is a sense in which the Church stands over against the world. There is a 'givenness' about the gospel, and this is not for sale in the interests of purchasing an accommodation with secular man. The basic question is this: Is the Church to base her life and teaching on the ideas and achievements of secular man, or on the revelation of God in Christ?

Moreover, just as it is true to say that orthodox Christianity has always been assailed in the name of advanced thought, so it is true that up till now orthodox Christianity has always survived. This fact should be taken more seriously than it usually is by those who are clamouring for an abandonment of traditional ways of thought. Further, most of the few advances being made by the Christian Church these days are being made by those who believe passionately in orthodox Christianity. Is not this a fact worthy of notice in modern thinking?

Addison H. Leitch makes much of this point in his discussion of the issues raised by *Honest to God*. He comments, 'if Robinson thinks that religion can be made palatable to 1963 any more than it was made palatable to the Roman Empire or to the Greek intelligentsia by a shift in terms, he is much misled. There is no Christianity without repentance of some kind, or strong crying and tears, and a kind of commitment to cross-bearing. These are the real stumbling-blocks. Meanwhile the tens of thousands come to hear Billy Graham. There is power in prayers to the God "out there," and there is power in preaching from the Bible as it is, not as reconstructed by Bultmann.'[8]

Sometimes a further error is made. The way some of its protagonists argue seems to imply that, if the case for

[8] *Christianity Today,* Nov. 8, 1963, p. 56.

Christianity is stated clearly enough, and if we refrain from importing into it traditional elements for which there is no warrant, then men will understand and probably accept it. Men will not accept orthodox Christianity. Let us then substitute something that they can understand and will accept.

But is this right? Men did not always understand Christ. And they did not accept Him. They crucified Him.

Men today have no right to expect that, if they are clear in their presentation of the essential message, and if this is freed from stumbling-blocks imported into it by the orthodox, men will respond. There is still such a thing as 'the offence of the cross' (Gal. 5: 11). It is not the way the cross is presented that is the basic reason for its rejection. That lies rather in the nature of the cross itself.

This can be made an excuse for intellectual and spiritual laziness by the orthodox. They can quote the text and then excuse themselves from doing anything about the fact that men do not respond to the gospel as they would like. This, of course, is tragic error. Wherever we see the gospel apparently ineffective we should agonize over the situation and search our hearts lest we be sinning in the way the new movement suggests, or in some other way. This must be quite clear. Evangelicals have no reason for complacency.

It must also be made quite clear that the Bible *does* speak of the offence of the cross. As far as I can see the new movement does not. Until it does it must be held to be defective in this aspect of Christianity at any rate. There is never any merit in seeking to evade the implications of the cross.

The new movement recognizes that the Christian Church has not always agreed with the attitude of the modern world to its discoveries and to itself. But it is usually said that the Church's attitude is wrong. Thus

Bonhoeffer sees something of the 'God of the gaps' attitude in the Church: 'Christian apologetic has taken the
most varying forms of opposition to this self-assurance.
Efforts are made to prove to a world thus come of age
that it cannot live without the tutelage of "God". Even
though there has been surrender on all secular problems,
there still remain the so-called ultimate questions—death,
guilt—on which only "God" can furnish an answer, and
which are the reason why God and the Church and the
pastor are needed. Thus we live, to some extent, by these
ultimate questions of humanity.'[9] Thus Bonhoeffer sees a
process of continual retreat. The Church has had to give
up its practice of seeing God as the explanation of
phenomena which are now satisfactorily explained by
science. And just as science has run the Church out of its
particular field, so have other disciplines removed the
necessity for postulating God in their respective fields.
Bonhoeffer sees the Church then as staking a last despair-
ing claim in the ultimate questions, the questions of death
and of guilt, where so far men not only have no solution,
but seem unlikely to provide the solution.

But Bonhoeffer is not willing to leave the matter there.
Seeing the process as he does, he will not rest content
with the usual ecclesiastical attitude. He goes on to ask
concerning these ultimate questions, 'But what if one
day they no longer exist as such, if they too can be
answered without "God"?'[1] He rejects with decision the
usual Christian approach to evangelism because he sees
in it the process we have just outlined. For him it is not
simply a setting forth of the truth of the Bible, but a
human contrivance, a way of trying to preserve ecclesiastical interests in the face of fears and massive secular
opposition. It is a negative tactic, a defensive ploy.

He rejects it out of hand. 'The attack by Christian
apologetic upon the adulthood of the world I consider to

[9] *Letters*, p. 107.
[1] *Loc. cit.*

be in the first place pointless, in the second ignoble, and in the third un-Christian. Pointless, because it looks to me like an attempt to put a grown-up man back into adolescence, *i.e.* to make him dependent on things on which he is not in fact dependent any more, thrusting him back into the midst of problems which are in fact not problems for him any more. Ignoble, because this amounts to an effort to exploit the weakness of man for purposes alien to him and not freely subscribed to by him. Un-Christian, because for Christ himself is being substituted one particular stage in the religiousness of man, i.e. a human law.'[2]

These are hard words. If they are justified then the Church must do a great deal of re-thinking of her mission. Much of her doctrine and much of her practice will have to be modified considerably.

But is the charge true? In the first place Bonhoeffer complains that what the Church is doing is pointless. This appears to mean that it is ineffective. Men will not listen to this kind of approach. They will reject it. Therefore we must abandon it.

But this hardly goes to the root of the matter. It has traditionally been regarded as the duty of the prophet to proclaim his message 'whether they will hear, or whether they will forbear' (Ezk. 2: 5,7). The prophet is commanded 'go . . . unto the children of thy people, and speak unto them, and tell them, Thus saith the Lord God; whether they will hear, or whether they will forbear' (Ezk. 3: 11). It is a new doctrine that the prophet is to abandon his uncompromising message when men merely regard it as outmoded. I do not find anywhere in Scripture justification for the view that a true prophet of God will modify his message simply because men find it unpalatable. In fact to adopt the latter course seems to be coming perilously close to what is denounced in the Scripture as the method of the false prophets.

[2] *Letters*, p. 108.

Bonhoeffer further complains that the Church's message about death and guilt is ignoble because it 'amounts to an effort to exploit the weakness of man'. But this is to put the lowest possible construction on it. It is fair to counter by asking, What is ignoble in calling on men to face facts? For death and guilt are facts. 'It is appointed unto men once to die', wrote the inspired author, and significantly he added, 'but after this the judgment' (Heb. 9: 27). Death is a reality. All men must face it. What does Bonhoeffer mean when he asks whether one day death may 'no longer exist as such'? Is he suggesting that men will find the means of making themselves immortal? If so, it is a somewhat precarious basis on which to erect theology. Or is he saying that men no longer fear death and that therefore God is not to be invoked in the face of it? If so, nothing much is gained. Fear it or not, men must die. Death is not a chimera, a phantom. It is real. It is surely the duty of the Christian theologian to face life as it is, and not as the pious expectation of the secular world hopes it one day may be. And right now death must be reckoned as a reality. We must talk to men on the basis that they will die.

Guilt too is a reality. I do not mean that all men necessarily feel guilty. It is quite obvious that they do not. The typical modern man, of whom Bonhoeffer writes so much, in his pride and self-sufficiency certainly does not feel himself to be a guilty person. But there is nothing new in this. From the time of the earliest prophets (and who knows for how long before that?) guilty men have lived brazenly denying their guilt. In fact it is just this attitude which calls forth the sternest denunciation of the prophets of the Old Testament and which is a continuing theme wherever men of God have faced it throughout the centuries. It is a new note, but one impossible to reconcile with biblical teaching, that it is ignoble to sheet home the world's guilt. E. L. Mascall

makes a relevant criticism of F. D. Maurice's position
(revived by A. R. Vidler in *Soundings*): 'The danger of
Maurice's attitude at the present day is that it may easily
be interpreted in the tempting form which assumes that
Christ came to tell us that we are really all right and that
therefore there is nothing to worry about, and may
therefore encourage a complacency which is every bit as
deadening as that against which Maurice was so violently
and laudably rebelling.'[3] Cannot this criticism be equally
urged against this aspect of Bonhoeffer's teaching?

It is un-Christian, says Bonhoeffer. Un-Christian to
take the teaching of Christ and apply it to our situation?
The fact must be faced that Jesus began His ministry by
saying, 'repent ye, and believe the gospel' (Mk. 1: 15).
Dealing with even the good actions of men He could say,
'If ye then, being evil . . . ' (Lk. 11: 13). He could call on
men to be converted if they would enter the kingdom
(Mt. 18: 3). Again and again He insisted that men must
reckon seriously with the evil that is in them, repent over
it and forsake it. How can teaching possibly be condemned as un-Christian when it simply follows Christ's
example in speaking bluntly of the sinfulness and guilt
of men and in calling on them to repent?

That Bonhoeffer was serious appears from his practice,
mentioned elsewhere. 'I often ask myself', he says, 'why
a Christian instinct frequently draws me more to the
religionless than to the religious, by which I mean not
with any intention of evangelising them, but rather, I
might almost say, in "brotherhood".'[4] This seems plain
enough. Bonhoeffer finds non-religious men to be already
in 'brotherhood'. He is more comfortable with them than
with the religious. Why should he challenge them?

There is a very revealing incident recorded concerning
an air raid. The prisoners were all lying on the floor and
one of them muttered, 'O God, O God'. Bonhoeffer

---

[3] *Up and Down in Adria* (London, 1963), p. 101.
[4] *Letters,* p. 92.

proceeds, 'I couldn't bring myself to offer him any Christian encouragement or comfort . . . perhaps I had a feeling that it was wrong to force religion down his throat just then.'[5] Most Christians would have felt that the situation called for a word of 'Christian encouragement or comfort'. Not so Bonhoeffer. He will not bring the gospel to a man who feels his need. That would be 'forcing religion down his throat'. Nor does he mention any further conversation with this man when his sense of need had passed. He gives no indication that the gospel is to be brought to the man under any circumstances. There is a curious attempt to justify his position by an example of Jesus. 'Incidentally, Jesus himself did not try to convert the two thieves on the cross; one of them turned to him.'[6] But the man he describes also turned to God, and called upon Him. Yet Bonhoeffer said no more to him than 'It won't last any more than ten minutes now'. His practice seems consistent with his theory.

I do not deny that passages can be found wherein Bonhoeffer speaks in general terms of claiming the secular world for Christ. Nor am I impugning his manner of life. In common I am sure with many others, I have felt the tepidity of my faith rebuked as I have read his burning letters from prison, and have caught revealing glimpses of a man who stood firm and was faithful even unto death. One who lives in easy circumstances has no business to complain about the martyrs. But the truth must be faced. The logic of Bonhoeffer's position appears to be that the secular world is not to be challenged to repent, and his letters give us no indication that he did in fact challenge it to repent.

It appears to be the same with some, at any rate, of his followers. Thus F. G. Downing has written an article entitled 'Man's Coming of Age'[7] in which he describes most appreciatively some of Bonhoeffer's views. As he comes to the end of the article he says, 'Adult or corrupt,

[5] *Letters,* p. 67.   [6] *Loc. cit.*   [7] *Prism,* Dec. 1962, pp. 31–42.

I cannot look for its weak points to force my religion on a non-religious world.'[8] Fair enough. No-one suggests that F. G. Downing's religion should be forced on a non-religious world. But who authorized F. G. Downing (or for that matter D. Bonhoeffer or J. A. T. Robinson) to tell the world that it need have nothing to do with *Christ's* religion? None of the new writers appears to give serious attention to the possibility that God may have chosen to give a definitive revelation of Himself in Christ. None of them troubles to examine, let alone refute, the claim that the Bible has a message for all men in all ages. Modern secular man is simply treated as a new species. He feels no need of God. Therefore he has no need of God. And therefore also there is no point in looking for Christ's teaching on the subject. Modern secular man is his own final authority. Thus it is that R. Gregor Smith can decline to demand that men be born again,[9] and can express some dissatisfaction with the answer given by Paul and Silas to the question, 'What must I do to be saved?'[1]

Repentance is an uncomfortable thing. Men have always sought to evade it, and not least among their evasions are those practised in the name of religion. But it is something new to suggest that it is no part of the Christian preacher's task when he stands over against the world to confront the world with the need to repent. If anything is to be termed un-Christian surely it is this

---

[8] *Op. cit.*, p. 41.

[9] *The New Man* (London, 1956), p. 83. His words are, 'nor should one distort the issue by demanding that they be born again in the strict evangelical connotation of recent generations'. These words could be understood to mean that there is a necessity for being born again, but that Evangelicals have misunderstood it. Smith, however, does not go on to show this. He speaks simply of the importance of living 'in openness and expectation of the possibility of being, in an emerging new community'. He leaves the impression that Evangelicals are in error in demanding that men be born again. And this with no reference at all to the meaning of John 3.

[1] *Op. cit.*, pp. 95 f.

new attitude. There is no note of challenge, no call on men to take the right way even though it be hard.

That is to say there is no challenge to men outside the Church. The new movement spends a great deal of time in rebuking orthodox Christianity. And as an orthodox Christian I sorrowfully accept the rebuke. Certainly the Church has often failed in its duty. Certainly it ought to be more thoughtful about what the essence of the gospel is, about how it can live by the gospel, and about how best to present the gospel to men living in the modern scientific age.

But does this, in fact, give the Church any justification for toning down the demands of Christ on others? If it is true that the Church must search its own heart it is also true that it must call on others to do the same with theirs. If it is true that it must repent of its own shortcomings it is true that it must call on the world to repent also.

One of the claims made incessantly by the new writers is that what they are doing is making the faith intelligible to modern man. That they intend to do this is undoubted. Whether they succeed is another matter. Modern man is often more perplexed by the novel teaching now being put before him than ever he was by orthodoxy. The vast majority of the lay people I have met who have read *Honest to God,* for example, express themselves as puzzled. They ask what the Bishop is trying to say. Whatever the truth of the positions put forward the book can scarcely claim to be successful as an essay in lucidity. The same is true of other writings. Thus H. W. Montefiore writes in *Soundings* about the nature of God, and E. L. Mascall can comment, 'I think that the man of the present day, when Mr. Montefiore says to him "I cannot go so far even as saying that God is a person; I must content myself with saying that God works in a personal way," is unlikely to feel that at last the Christian religion is being presented to him in a way that he can understand

and, on the strength of it, rush to offer himself for
baptism. I think he is more likely to recoil in dismay and
flee into the arms of Dr. Waddington or of Chalcedon.'[2]

Many of the reactions to *Honest to God* show clearly
enough that, though that book has had wide acceptance,
it has not succeeded in making the gospel intelligible.
Thus Fenton Morley, in his article in the *Sunday
Telegraph* in which he gives an account of reactions to
the book within the Church of England, cites this summary of its teaching from 'a rare attender' at church:
'God is unknowable. Love equals Jesus. All life is prayer
—so why bother to come to church?'[3] Morley cites
another reaction: 'One of the very few reports of any
awareness came from a factory hand who is a committed
Christian. "What I get in the canteen," he said, "is that
they always said there isn't a personal God, and now one
of the bishops has said so too!" In spite of the publicity
Honest to God seems to have failed to get through to the
man in the cloth cap.'[4]

It may also not be without significance that Bishop
Robinson has been so persistently charged with atheism.
Especially serious is the article by Alasdair Macintyre
which begins, 'What is striking about Dr Robinson's
book is first and foremost that he is an atheist.'[5] Later he
says, 'So the bishop is fundamentally at one with Hume
and Feuerbach, and at odds with Aquinas, Luther, and
Billy Graham';[6] 'if Dr Robinson's argument is right, the
traditional views of God are not merely outmoded; they
are simply false.'[7] The Bishop of Woolwich defends himself against the accusation, but Leslie Paul does not find
the reply satisfactory.[8]

This book is meant to state Christianity in a way which

[2] *Op. cit.*, p. 73.   [3] *HTGD*, p. 46.
[4] *Loc. cit.*   [5] *HTGD*, p. 215.   [6] *HTGD*, p. 216.
[7] *HTGD*, p. 216, n. 1. *Cf.* also the views of T. E. Utley,
(*HTGD*, p. 95), David Boulton (*HTGD*, pp. 106 f.), Antony
Flew (*HTGD*, p. 145), Julian Huxley (*HTGD*, p. 175).
[8] *View Review*, November 1963, p. 22.

will prove acceptable to modern men. But it is not only *possible* that men may think its author an atheist, men *actually have* been led to this conclusion. Since this has happened the book cannot be said to be clear. Nor can it be called satisfactory, for surely the very last thing that Christians want to do is to give the impression that they are commending atheism.

Part of the reason for the book's being misunderstood in so curious a fashion may be that the Bishop of Woolwich has not yet become clear in his own mind as to what he is trying to say. He tells us that he is trying 'to think aloud', and he can say, 'I am struggling to think other people's thoughts after them. I cannot claim to have understood all I am trying to transmit.'[9] This is said with candour and humility, and, indeed, his whole book is permeated with such a spirit. But if the writer himself does not understand it, it is asking a lot for his readers to find what he is saying perspicuous.

Bishop Robinson's confession may give us the clue to some of those difficulties wherein he appears to be saying two opposite things. Thus on one and the same page he can say of a certain way of thinking about God, 'There is nothing intrinsically wrong with it,' and, 'I am firmly convinced that this whole way of thinking can be the greatest obstacle to an intelligent faith—and indeed will progressively be so to all except the "religious" few.'[1] If

---

[9] *HTG*, p. 21. On these words J. D. Douglas says, 'He might profess not to know what the message was when it left him, but when it gets to us it seems perilously like a major and determined attack upon Christian orthodoxy' (*Christianity Today*, June 21, 1963, p. 48). Bonhoeffer is another who tells us that he is not clear on what he is trying to say. More than once he says that he is writing to try to clear his mind, or that he is thinking aloud or the like (*Letters*, pp. 95, 119). He can even say, 'I find it's very slow going trying to work out a non-religious interpretation of biblical terminology, and it's a far bigger job than I can manage at the moment' (*Letters*, p. 120). He speaks of being 'led on more by an instinctive feeling for the questions which are bound to crop up rather than by any conclusions I have reached already' (*Letters*, p. 106).   [1] *HTG*, p. 43.

I understand him aright, he is here saying that this way of thinking about God is not wrong, but that nevertheless it is quite possible for it to be a very great obstacle to intelligent men now, and, as the days go by, it will become such an obstacle for the great majority of men. But I do not see how a way of thinking which is now an obstacle to the intelligent, and in the future will be an obstacle to all but a few, can be anything other than wrong.

No wonder some find it difficult to see what the Bishop means here. If the traditional way of thinking about God is not wrong why is he calling on us to abandon it? Or is he calling on us to abandon it? If not, why does he keep telling us that in the future only a tiny minority will be content to retain it? Such uncertainties as these in points of major importance, in a book which professes to point us to a clearer understanding of the essence of the faith, leave many readers perplexed and sad. Perhaps Dr. Robinson is trying to say something very important. But what is it?

While we are thinking about the difficulty of getting his meaning we might turn our attention to his teaching on prayer, for it is possible that this section of the book shows us one reason why so many places are so very hard to understand. 'Prayer', he tells us, 'is the responsibility to meet others with *all* I have, to be ready to encounter the unconditional in the conditional, to expect to meet God in the way, not to turn aside from the way.'[2] Now with all respect, this is not what prayer is. It is finely said, and the practice commended is undoubtedly worthy. But it is not prayer. By calling it prayer Dr. Robinson is surely confusing the issue. It would be better if he said something like this: 'Prayer as it has always been practised is no longer to be commended, at least for some people. It would be much better to follow this new practice.' Then we would know where we were. But it does not help to have quite a new practice labelled with the old name

[2] *HTG*, p. 100.

'Prayer'. That leaves us uncertain and it obscures the meaning. And if the Bishop uses a word here in a sense it does not normally bear, the suspicion arises that perhaps he has done the same elsewhere, and that this is why he leaves us confused.[3]

The curious use of language in the Bishop's book moves O. Fielding Clarke to say, 'This Pickwickian use of everyday words is of course the besetting sin of "Oxbridge".' He goes on to point out that dons 'are apt to lose the common touch, and never more perilously than when they imagine that they at least are not as other dons are—"remote and ineffectual," as certain also of our own poets have said'. He complains of 'this itch to use ordinary words in extraordinary senses without apparently a thought for what this can mean to the man in the street'.[4] This protest seems completely justified. It is important to use words in a way which can be understood, and it is difficult to acquit the Bishop of Woolwich of taking certain words and using them in a way that is highly unusual, to say the least of it.

It is all the more curious that he should do this in that he is certainly trying very hard to make the essence of the Christian faith known to modern man, and more

---

[3] Bonhoeffer can also give old terminology a new sense. He tells us that *metanoia* 'is not in the first instance bothering about one's own needs, problems, sins, and fears, but allowing oneself to be caught up in the way of Christ, into the Messianic event, and thus fulfilling Isaiah 53' (*Letters*, p. 123; note incidentally the way being caught up in Christ's way is immediately interpreted in terms of the Old Testament!). Now the attitude Bonhoeffer is inculcating is an attitude which should characterize Christians. It is right and necessary. But that is no reason for calling it repentance. 'Repentance' is a word with a meaning of its own, and no good purpose is served by retaining the word and abandoning the meaning. That way lies confusion. In passing it is worth noticing that in *The Cost of Discipleship* (London, 1959) he could say, 'Cheap grace is the preaching of forgiveness without requiring repentance. . . . Cheap grace is grace without discipleship, grace without the cross' (*op. cit.*, p. 36). That is surely the condemnation of 'religionless Christianity'.

[4] *For Christ's Sake* (London, 1963), pp. 27 f.

especially to modern scientific man. But to use words in this way will certainly not help in achieving this aim. It is much more likely that modern man will be impressed if Christians take the trouble to use their words carefully, with precise meanings. Scientific man is not in the habit of using words in bewilderingly new senses, at least not without a careful explanation of what he is about. It may be significant that not a few of those scientists who are Christians are orthodox Christians. To cite O. Fielding Clarke again, 'Incidentally, *why* does Dr. Robinson (who is not a scientist) imagine that science-trained people find his chosen mentors so illuminating? The odd thing is that, so often, the scientists who *are* Christians are orthodox. Could it be that they prefer a precise concrete language which, even if it needs translating, at least has a definable sense to start with?'[5] The question bears thinking through. I do not think that it has been proved that modern man rejects the essential gospel because the orthodox expression of it is too hard for him to understand.

That the Church has failed to make the gospel relevant to modern man is obvious enough. But why is this? Sometimes the theologians of whom we are thinking appear to hold that it is because we have not put the gospel in the right words, and sometimes it seems that they are trying to say that it is because we do not believe the right things. We are holding on to the ideas of an earlier age which we dub 'Christian' and we fail to perceive that the modern world has passed on and that it will never again hold these beliefs.

But it is open to question whether either of these really gets to the heart of the matter. Is it not true that the greatest fault has been in our living, not in our believing or expressing? We have given at best a very imperfect

---

[5] *Op. cit.*, p. 20. Similarly J. W. C. Wand says, 'The few top-ranking scientists one has met would probably prefer the precision of traditional belief' (*HTGD*, p. 86).

picture of what constitutes the Christian life and the
world has not been attracted by it. But here and there,
where men have been living out the implications of their
faith, they have usually been successful in commending
the gospel to those around them. This is not to say that
all is well either with our manner of expressing the gospel
or with our understanding of what the gospel is. Both
leave much to be desired. But neither is so far adrift that
Christianity could not become a live option for the men
of our day if only it appeared an attractive faith in the
lives of those who profess it. But Christian practice all
too often falls woefully short of Christian profession, and
this cannot but affect our impact on the world. Those
who hold to the need for a 'religionless Christianity'
might perhaps do well to give some thought to the difference made by the indifferent way most of us live the
religious life.

Since the orthodox may well feel that they have no
reason for pride in their achievement it is perhaps worth
asking whether the new movement can do better. But if
we apply the test, 'by their fruits ye shall know them', it
scarcely scores a notable triumph. It does not even ask
men to be different. One of the curious things about it
all is that, despite the widespread interest that has been
aroused, little change appears to have been brought about
in people. *The Honest to God Debate* cites a number
of letters from people who have read *Honest to God,* but
in no case does a writer say that he was challenged by
the book and has altered his life as a result. The best we
get is that people feel 'liberated'. But when we look into
this they appear to mean that they have had a certain
way of life that was not, they thought, Christian. Now
that they have read the Bishop's book they find that it is
(*cf.* the woman who wrote, 'It is just so marvellous to
have all this coming from a bishop of the Church, and
having one's thoughts and hopes confirmed'[6]). They con-

* *HTGD,* p. 55.

tinue to live as they did before, but now they can think of themselves as Christians. This can scarcely be thought of as a successful venture in evangelism.

Perhaps it is not surprising, for the Bishop himself tells us that he looks for no converts. He cites Leslie Mitton's words: 'The book is fundamentally not an essay in unorthodox theology, but a venture in evangelism.' He proceeds, 'I accept that. But it is a venture in evangelism with a difference. It is not addressed from inside the Church to those outside—I have not mustered arguments to "convert" anyone.'[7] This is indeed evangelism 'with a difference', another example of using great Christian words with a new meaning. Traditionally 'evangelism' has meant proclaiming the gospel in such a way as to bring men to saving faith in Christ. But this new evangelism is apparently content to leave them where they are. All that it does is to assure them that their secularism is not as anti-Christian as they had feared. It is not surprising that T. E. Utley can say, 'It is not always clear, indeed, whether the Bishop's aim is to convince agnostics that they can conscientiously go to church or to persuade Christians that there is no real need to do so.'[8]

It is this aspect of the new movement that causes Kl. Runia to express his doubts as to whether this is the way to bring the gospel to the modern intellectual. 'No doubt it will appeal to him', says Runia. 'But will he find the gospel in it? We cannot possibly see how he ever would, for there is no gospel in this philosophy! It is only a new world-view which, as such, may assist modern man in finding more coherence and depth in the perplexing multitude of phenomena and experiences. But it cannot

[7] *HTGD*, p. 275.
[8] *HTGD*, p. 97. He adds, 'At the lowest, he seems to me to be violating the principles of honest commerce by trying to sell as Christian a commodity that bears no relation to the historical and accepted meaning of that word.'

save, because it does not contain the saving power of the Christian gospel.'[9]

Let this statement be carefully thought through. Evangelicals are not opposed to the modern movement out of hidebound conservatism. No doubt they are slow to change, perhaps too slow. But that is not because they fear progress. It is because they are sure that 'God was in Christ, reconciling the world unto himself' (2 Cor. 5: 19), and they are sure that this is integral to Christianity. They cannot abandon this sure word of the gospel and they cannot embrace a movement which fails to safeguard this truth. They do not see it safeguarded in *Honest to God,* nor in most of the other books with which we are here concerned. That is the cause for their concern.

This must be made as clear as it can be. It is not some conventional, human statement of the gospel for which I am contending. It does not matter whether the way I proclaim the gospel, or for that matter the way any other Evangelical proclaims it, is preserved or not. But it matters everything that the gospel be preserved. If those who uphold 'religionless Christianity' wish to commend their view to Evangelicals it will not be by showing that it is congenial to modern philosophers, or scientists, or to the intelligentsia generally. It will be by showing that in it is an authentic restatement of the essential truth of the gospel. At present it does not look as though men are being told that none of their own efforts can save them but only the grace of God. It looks as though men are being told to live their secular lives to the full. And that is not the gospel.

This is how the Bishop of Woolwich sees Christian

[9] *I Believe in God* (London, 1963), p. 71. Runia's charge that the new movement is not authentic Christianity but a modern version of Gnosticism (*op. cit.,* pp. 60 f.) is seriously stated, and is worthy of close examination. It is not easy to see how it can be refuted.

duty: 'In morals, as in everything else, "the secret of our exit" from the morasses of relativism is not, I believe, a "recall to religion", a reassertion of the sanctions of the supranatural. It is to take our place alongside those who are deep in the search for meaning *etsi deus non daretur,* even if God is not "there". It is to join those on the Emmaus road who have no religion left, and there, in, with and under the meeting of man with man and the breaking of our common bread, to encounter the unconditional as the Christ of our lives.'[1] Putting aside the slur on those who walked the road to Emmaus (what possible justification is there for saying that they had no religion left?), this statement appears to mean that Christians should not try to recall men to religion. Rather they should join those who have no religion, even though God is not 'there'. Is this evangelism or surrender?

The new movement, then, can scarcely be called a highly successful venture in communication. So many of us find ourselves unable to say for certain what it is that it is saying. Great old words are used with novel meanings and without any explanation of what is being done. Apparently contradictory ideas are set side by side with no word of reconciliation. Small wonder that the effect that is conveyed to many is that the theologians are now saying that there is no God and that we are all all right.

It is more than difficult to see it as a successful experiment in evangelism. Authentic notes of the gospel are missing or muted. It lacks the note of challenge. It seems to be intent on telling secular man that he is all right where and as he is. There is no call for him to repent and believe. He is not faced with the demand that he take up his cross and follow Christ.

[1] *HTG,* p. 121.

CHAPTER EIGHT

IS 'RELIGIONLESS CHRISTIANITY' REALLY CHRISTIAN?

THE reviewer of Dr. Robinson's book in *The Times* said, among other things, 'the doubt is whether what he retains amounts to Christianity'. Certainly it is not what men through nineteen centuries have understood by Christianity. Christianity has always had certain views about the nature of God and the nature of man. It has seen God as an all-powerful Person, a Person who is not only loving but who is love, who took action for sinful man and provided for his salvation by the way of the cross. It has seen man as sinful. It has not regarded pride and self-sufficiency as matters to be lauded, but to be denounced.

But now, as I understand it, we are asked to see man as come of age, to see 'religion' as an error and a delusion and to see the truly Christian way as refusing to assert 'the sanctions of the supranatural' and as simply a taking up one's position among those who have no religion left. Well may J. I. Packer say, 'So the real Christian life, whatever else it is, is precisely *not* the life of faith in the living Lord, of believing His promises and obeying His orders, which Abraham and Moses and David and Elijah and Jeremiah and Paul and Augustine and Luther and Tyndale and Wesley and Hudson Taylor and George Müller and the Auca martyrs of our own day lived. Here, then, is a dilemma; *either* those in the heroes' gallery of Hebrews 11, and the millions more who have lived and died by "faith" as there defined, were really deluded, and the knowledge of God which they thought they had was unreal, *or else* the Tillich-Robinson "theology" is not theology, and their "God" is not God, and their "prayer" is not prayer, and their "worship" is not worship.'[1]

One consequence of the rejection of 'the sanctions of the supranatural' and the rest of orthodox Christianity is that what remains has little resemblance to what has always been understood to be essential Christianity. Here, for example, are some words which A. R. Vidler quotes from an anonymous Anglican missionary : 'This way perhaps lies a solution to the problem that Arnold Toynbee has pressed in "Christianity among the Religions"—the intolerance implied, and the quarrels inevitable, when "Christianity" claims to be the only true religion. If we are content to admit that Christianity is more or less indistinguishable from the other religions in matters of theology, priests, prayers, sacraments, etc., and that a man can as well become a disciple of Jesus and use his words to interpret the Five Principles of Confucius as he can use them to interpret the Ten Commandments, if we have the courage to leave the appeal of Jesus to the conscience and the aesthetic sense —to the Holy Ghost—then we have what? We have apostasy, heresy, horror — everything that the true churchman instinctively recoils from—but that does not mean that we do not have Jesus Christ, if only he were sufficient for us.'[2]

I do not think that this writer is going much, if at all, beyond what other writers of this school say and imply. By sitting loose to the distinctives of Christianity it is fairly obvious that they are drawing near to the other

---

[1] *Keep Yourselves from Idols* (London, 1963), pp. 8 f. Similarly E. L. Mascall complains of the view of H. A. Williams that Christians have not hitherto understood how and when to give themselves in love, that 'it is equivalent to saying that the great saints and teachers of Christendom have been uniformly mistaken in their notions of the way in which a life of Christian commitment was to be lived and that nobody knew how and when to give himself until the time of Freud' (*Up and Down in Adria*, London, 1963, p. 41).

[2] *Soundings*, pp. 249 f.

religions of the world. But what he is doing is something which for the most part they do not face—he is admitting that this new view is 'apostasy, heresy, horror'. He goes on to the thought that this does not mean 'that we do not have Jesus Christ', but he does not seek in the slightest to modify the suggestion that he is putting forward heresy. His views may be right or they may be wrong, but the point is that they are not Christianity. The fact must be faced that in this new movement, despite the vigorous protestations of some of its protagonists, we are being asked to accept not a re-stated version of Christianity, a Christianity translated into the idiom of the twentieth century, but a new heresy, an apostasy. It is a religion which can speak of the Five Principles of Confucius alongside the Ten Commandments. One wonders whether the Epistle to the Hebrews was written in vain.

It is perhaps in line with the views of his correspondent that Vidler himself can view with disapprobation a situation in which 'The Church of England would be cleaned up and tidied up, so that everyone could tell just what it stood for. It is premature for any church to try to put itself in that position.'[3] While one can understand a man who welcomes the comprehension of the Church of England and its ready tolerance of a wide range of opinion, I find it curious that an eminent theologian can publicly disclaim the view that a church ought to make plain what it stands for. And I do not see how this kind of attitude can be reconciled to one which says that the new movement is making Christianity more intelligible to the men of our day. If Vidler's position is to be accepted it is doing nothing of the sort. It is telling those men that even the Church does not know what it stands for. And if it does not, then it is hard indeed to see why they should have any interest in what it has to say.

A curious exception to the tolerance shown in general

[3] *Soundings*, p. 261.

by the new writers is their attitude to old-fashioned conservatives. They speak warmly of the world and its autonomy, they welcome with open arms (though admitting the errors of) the liberal movement, and even Roman Catholicism and the Orthodox Church. But when they speak of conservatives it is to say such things as, 'This lack, which is really a pervasive lovelessness, is apparent in the whole fundamentalist apprehension of the Word of God and the intention of Christianity. The world is denied by such an apprehension. It is set at a distance, and the space between the avowed fundamentalist Christian and the world is not filled, as it can be, and must be, by the action of understanding love.'[4]

This is nothing less than irresponsible. It betrays Gregor Smith's complete ignorance of what he calls 'fundamentalist'. I am not concerned to defend the fundamentalists. Among them, as among other Christians, there are those lacking in love and limited in vision. But to characterize the whole movement as loveless can, in my judgment, proceed only from ignorance or prejudice. The best fundamentalists I know have just as sure a grasp of the truth that all of life is God's and that the world is God's world as is revealed in Smith's book. And the best of them live lives so characterized by love as to put others to shame. To overlook this and to berate these devoted servants of God is to render a notable disservice to truth.

It is striking that so little attempt is made by adherents of the new way of thinking to justify their position by showing that it is in accordance with the New Testament. One would have thought this fundamental for a movement that professes to set out the very essence of Christianity. But it proves not to be the case. Often the argument proceeds from general principles. And when appeal is made to the Bible a surprising thing emerges. Often it is the Old Testament rather than the New that

[4] R. Gregor Smith, *op. cit.*, p. 77.

receives the emphasis. This is so with Bonhoeffer himself in those parts of his writings where he is concerned to set forth religionless Christianity. It is not so in his earlier works, such as *The Cost of Discipleship,* or his *Ethics,* but in the *Letters and Papers from Prison* where he puts forward his ideas about the new shape of Christianity there is certainly much more interest in the Old Testament than in the New. This is to be discerned in the total number of texts quoted, for the index shows that his Old Testament quotations far outnumber those from the New Testament (which is not the case in his earlier writings). And it is not simply a matter of citing numbers of texts. The thought is often dominated by the Old Testament, sometimes in explicit opposition to the New.

Thus he writes to a friend, 'My thoughts and feelings seem to be getting more and more like the Old Testament, and no wonder, I have been reading it much more than the New for the last few months. It is only when one knows the ineffability of the Name of God that one can utter the name of Jesus Christ. It is only when one loves life and the earth so much that without them everything would be gone, that one can believe in the resurrection and a new world. . . . I don't think it is Christian to want to get to the New Testament too soon and too directly. . . . Why is it that in the Old Testament men lie so frequently and on such a grand scale to the glory of God (I have collected together all the instances), that they commit murder, trickery, robbery, adultery and even whoredom (see the genealogy of Jesus), that they doubt, blaspheme and curse, whereas there is no sign of these things in the New Testament? It's easy to say that the Old Testament represents an earlier stage of religious evolution, but that is too naïve, for after all it is the same God in both Testaments.'[5]

It is arguable that Bonhoeffer is not being quite fair to either Testament in this passage. But it is quite clear

[5] *Letters,* p. 50.

that he is basing his position, and that explicitly, on the Old Testament rather than the New. It is there that he sees the love of 'life and the world' that means so much to him as we see throughout this book. This is not peripheral. It is the seeing of God in the common life which is central to the whole idea of religionless Christianity. It is important to see that for Bonhoeffer, whatever may be true of others, this is essentially an Old Testament idea, and that he puts it forth in a context wherein he expresses himself in no hurry to get through to the New Testament.

And even when he professes to set out the teaching of the New Testament he commonly takes the Old Testament as decisive and interprets the New in the light of it. Thus he can ask 'Is there any concern in the Old Testament about saving one's soul at all?' and go on, 'Is not righteousness and and the kingdom of God on earth the focus of everything . . . ?'[6] Then he proceeds to the New Testament to find the same teaching.

The topic of salvation is found elsewhere. Thus Bonhoeffer says, 'Unlike the other oriental religions the faith of the Old Testament is not a religion of salvation. Christianity, it is true, has always been regarded as a religion of salvation. But isn't this a cardinal error, which divorces Christ from the Old Testament and interprets him in the light of the myths of salvation?'[7] Christ, it appears, is to be interpreted in the light of the Old Testament and not *vice versa*. But, if the two Testaments are to be separated in this way why should the Old have the prescriptive right?

Bonhoeffer goes on to the idea of the resurrection. 'It is said that the distinctive feature of Christianity is its proclamation of the resurrection hope, and that this means the establishment of a genuine religion of salvation, in the sense of release from this world. The emphasis falls upon the far side of the boundary drawn by

* *Letters*, p. 94.   ⁷ *Letters*, p. 112.

death. But this seems to me to be just the mistake and the danger. Salvation means salvation from cares and need, from fears and longing, from sin and death into a better world beyond the grave. But is this really the distinctive feature of Christianity as proclaimed in the Gospels and St. Paul? I am sure it is not. The difference between the Christian hope of resurrection and a mythological hope is that the Christian hope sends a man back to his life on earth in a wholly new way which is even more sharply defined than it is in the Old Testament.'[8]

Certainly the Christian hope does send a man back to this life to live it out to the full. But the point for us to notice here is that Bonhoeffer rests his argument not on the New Testament, but in the first place on general considerations and in the second on what he conceives to be the teaching of the Old Testament.

A little later he deals with his correspondent's doubts. 'So you think the Bible has very little to say about health, fortune, vigour, etc. That is certainly not true of the Old Testament.' (Notice how Bonhoeffer immediately goes to the Old Testament.) 'The intermediate theological category between God and human fortune is, it seems to me, that of blessing. There is indeed no concern for fortune in the Old Testament, but there is a concern for the blessing of God, which includes all earthly blessings as well. In this blessing the whole of earthly life is claimed for God, and all his promises are included in it.'[9] He thinks that 'It would be natural to suppose that as usual the New Testament spiritualizes the teaching of the Old at this point, and that therefore the Old Testament blessing is superseded in the New', but against this cites the mention of sickness and death in connection with misuse of the Lord's Supper (1 Cor. 10: 16; 11: 30), Jesus' restoration of men to health and the fact that His disciples while with Him lacked nothing. He concludes :

[8] *Letters*, p. 112.   [9] *Letters*, pp. 126 f.

'The only difference between the two Testaments at this
point is that in the Old the blessing also includes the
cross, and in the New the cross also includes the blessing.'[1]
Many will welcome this way of putting it, and I am not
concerned to quarrel with the conclusion. What I do
want to point out is that it is not reached by way of a
careful evaluation of New Testament teaching. It is
reached by way of making a generalization from the Old
Testament, and then going on to see whether something
might be found in the New Testament to support it. The
Old Testament is determinative.

And this apparently corresponds to a deeply held
conviction. Thus when he is offering his friend seven
suggestions for a text on which to preach he takes six
of them from the Old Testament.[2] And when he is
writing his 'Thoughts on the Baptism of D.W.R.', surely
a document composed in deep earnestness and with a
serious attempt to convey what seems to him to be of the
chief importance, he makes nineteen quotations from
Scripture of which no less than sixteen are from the Old
Testament.[3] Or we might cite the passage in which he
refers to the Song of Songs, 'and one could hardly have
a more passionate and sensual love than is there por-
trayed (see 7. 6). It is a good thing that that book is
included in the Bible as a protest against those who
believe that Christianity stands for the restraint of
passion (is there any example of such restraint anywhere
in the Old Testament?).'[4] This last is most illuminating.
He cites those who maintain that a certain belief is
Christian. But he protests against this position on the
grounds that it is not to be found in the Old Testament.
We could scarcely have a more illuminating passage for
the revelation of what is primary with Bonhoeffer at this
time, all the more so since his reference is so incidental.
He is not trying to impress anyone or to be formal. He

[1] *Letters*, p. 127.
[3] *Letters*, pp. 154–160.
[2] *Letters*, p. 120.
[4] *Letters*, p. 100.

is simply going to that which he sees as most significant for a solution to his problem.

All this does not mean that appeal should not be made to the Old Testament. I hope I hold the Old Testament to be sacred Scripture in as real and as serious a way as did Bonhoeffer. It is certainly part of the Word of God, and it must not be neglected or depreciated.

But neither must it be elevated to the place where it is given the supreme place in the determination of *Christian* doctrine. For that we must turn to Christ and His apostles. We must not neglect the Old Testament, but we must interpret it in the light of the fuller revelation of the New, and not *vice versa*. Christ is central to Christianity. It is distressing that so eminent a theologian and so brave a martyr as Bonhoeffer should in his last days concentrate on the Old Testament to such an extent that Christ is brought in only to confirm what has already been discovered in the Old Testament. And it is also distressing that so many recent writers who have hailed Bonhoeffer's work and who are claiming to go on in the way he has pioneered have not realized how little of the New Testament is in what he is writing (or if they have realized it have not said so).

All this casts a doubt on whether 'religionless Christianity' can rightly claim to be Christian at all. If it is a system which depends in the last resort on a particular interpretation of the Old Testament then why should we call it 'religionless Christianity' rather than, say, 'religionless Judaism'? I do not think it has yet been demonstrated that the new movement is really impregnated with the mind of Christ.

It is true that sometimes it is made to sound orthodox, as when Dr. Robinson says, 'Christianity stands or falls by revelation, by Christ as the disclosure of the final truth not merely about human nature (that we might accept relatively easily) but about all nature and all reality . . . the Christian's faith is in Christ as the revelation, the laying bare, of the very heart and being of ultimate reality.'[5] This is finely said, and it will surely be endorsed whole-heartedly by orthodox Christians. But they will go on to ask, Where has Dr. Robinson tried to show that his new system originates in the revelation made in Jesus Christ? Where has he succeeded in showing even that it is compatible with that revelation? It is not enough to acknowledge the primary place of God's revelation in Christ. It is necessary also to erect one's theology on that basis and not on a basis of an un-critical acceptance of the modern man's world view. It is because the theologians of whom we are thinking so often give the impression that this is what they are doing that their work creates so profound a sense of disap-pointment. If their work is to be called 'Christian' in any meaningful senses it will be necessary to show that it stems from Christ. To date this has not been done.[6]

Nels Ferré has a criticism of Tillich and Bultmann which is more widely relevant. He says, 'For a time, Tillich and Bultmann were interpreted as merely modernizing the faith in terms of the demythologizing of outworn world-views. Then many began to question the relation between myth, symbol and reality in their systems. Finally, it is becoming more and more obvious that *ontologically* the whole Christian interpretation and offer of salvation are not only radically altered and shrunk, but in fact surrendered.'[7] No-one questions the sincerity of such men as Tillich and Bultmann, or for that matter, of Bonhoeffer and Robinson. But sincerity is not enough. As Ferré points out, the systems of the first two

[5] *HTG*, p. 128.
[6] R. C. Lucas, in an account of two lunch-hour talks given at St. Helen's Church, Bishopsgate, says of *Honest to God* that 'its presentation of the Faith is neither Biblical, Christian nor Angli-can'. There is no denying that this is the impression that has been given to very many.
[7] *Searchlights on Contemporary Theology* (New York, 1961), p. 91.

do represent a surrender of important elements of the Christian faith. And the same appears to many to be true also of the latter two. There is thus serious doubt as to whether the new movement retains the essential gospel. Many of its exponents say it does. But they have yet to show that what they are saying is in essentials the same as the gospel of Christ. In many points their teaching is demonstrably taken from the Old Testament, with some attempt to show that the New Testament does not contradict it. But in no place known to me does any of these writers really get to grips with the gospel as a revealed message centring on a divine action for man's salvation.

This movement might have been a mighty force in making the gospel known to this generation. It boasts outstanding names. It puts forth exciting ideas. But as at present set forth it seems that everywhere it comes under the condemnation put so concisely by St. Paul, 'then is the offence of the cross ceased' (Gal. 5: 11).

to represent a surrender of important elements of the Christian faith. And the same appears to many to be true also of the latter two. There is thus serious doubt as to whether the new movement retains the essential gospel. Many of its exponents say it does. But they have yet to show that what they are saying is in essentials the same as the gospel of Christ. In many points their teaching is debatably taken from the Old Testament, with some attempt to show that the New Testament does not contradict it. But in no place known to me does any of these writers really get to grips with the gospel as a revealed message centring on a divine action for man's salvation.

This movement might have been a mighty force in making the gospel known to this generation. It boasts outstanding names. It puts forth exciting ideas. But at present it seems it seems that everywhere it comes under the condemnation put so cogently by St. Paul, 'then is the offence of the cross ceased' (Gal. 5: 11).